Dear C

It is an honor meeting you! May you continue to shine + flourish through Christ Jesus, in Jesus name!

Ps. 92:12

Love,
Kim

A GUIDE TO BECOMING
A **BOLDER** AND BETTER YOU

SPEAK
Submit
SURRENDER

KIMBERLY SANON

Speak Submit Surrender

Copyright © 2021 by Kimberly Sanon - All Rights Reserved. The moral rights of the author have been asserted. No part of this book may be reproduced in any form by an electronic or mechanical means, including information storage and retrieval systems, without permission in writing from the publisher, except by a reviewer who may quote brief passages in a review.

This edition: ISBN 978-0-578-75798-8 (softcover)

Published by Equipping Arrows Enterprise LLC.
Equipping Arrows Enterprise LLC.
equippingarrows@gmail.com
www.equippingarrowsenterprise.com

Cover Design by Gloria Owusu
www.ashelecreative.com

About the Author Photograph, Copyright © 2020 – 2021 by Pascale Mobley - All Rights Reserved.
www.pascalelourdes.com
Interior book designer by HoneyPino from fiverr.com

Scripture quotations marked (NLT) and unmarked are taken from the Holy Bible, New Living Translation, copyright ©1996, 2004, 2015 by Tyndale House Foundation. Used by permission of Tyndale House Publishers, Carol Stream, Illinois 60188. All rights reserved.

Scripture quotations marked (TPT) are taken from the Holy Bible, The Passion Translation®. Copyright © 2017 by BroadStreet Publishing® Group, LLC. Used by permission. All rights reserved. thePassionTranslation.com

Scripture quotations marked (AMP) taken from the Amplified® Bible (AMP), Copyright © 2015 by The Lockman Foundation. Used by permission. www.lockman.org

Scripture quotations marked (NKJV) taken from the New King James Version®. Copyright © 1982 by Thomas Nelson. Used by permission. All rights reserved.

Scripture quotations marked (BSB) taken from the Berean Bible (www.Berean.Bible) Berean Study Bible (BSB) © 2016, 2020 by Bible Hub and Berean.Bible. Used by Permission. All rights Reserved.

Scripture quotations marked (VOICE) taken from the Voice Bible Copyright © 2012 Thomas Nelson, Inc. The Voice™ translation © 2012 Ecclesia Bible Society All rights reserved.

Disclaimer: The names and some details have been changed or omitted to protect the privacy of individuals mentioned within this book. The views, thoughts, and opinions expressed in this book belong solely to the author and not to the author's employer, other groups, any persons, corporations and/or organizations associated with the author. The content within this book does not serve as a replacement for any forms of advice, counseling, therapy, consulting, etc. This book is also not liable for any forms of damages. If you or someone you know is in any type of danger, please seek help immediately.

Thank You

A special thank you to the lover of my soul, my Lord and Savior, Jesus Christ! Thank You for being My Everything! I love and honor You! Thank You for loving me first! It is an honor to do Your will for such a time as this for Your glory alone! Thank you to Jesus' beautiful bride, His Church, The Body of Christ! To my brothers and sisters in Christ, I love and thank God for each and every one of you! Thank you for your obedience unto God and releasing every prayer, sermon, blessing, word of encouragement, hospitable act, prophetic utterance, correction, and kind words over my family and I. May the Lord continue to bless you and keep you, may the Lord make His face shine upon you and be gracious to you, may the Lord turn His face toward you and give you peace (Numbers 6:24-26) in Jesus mighty name!

Dedication

I would like to dedicate this book to every woman, daughter, mother, sister, aunt, and every person who has been silenced told that they were crazy or been overwhelmed with hopelessness, shame, and depression. There is much more to your life than the lies whispered in your ear. God didn't create you to live life belittled. You were created for such a time as this! It is time to walk into your true identity and God-given destiny! It is time for you to be BOLD!

Contents

Introduction x

Section I Speak

Chapter 1   Dark Days in December 2
Chapter 2   Face to Face 6
Chapter 3   Crisis At Hand 10
Chapter 4   Unmuzzled 16

Section II Submit

Chapter 5   The Escape Plan 24
Chapter 6   Overcoming Trauma 29
Chapter 7   Obedience over Everything 34
Chapter 8   Stand out in Character 40
Chapter 9   Moving in Faith 44
Chapter 10 Answer The Call 52

Section III Surrender

Chapter 11 Purpose and Prudence 60
Chapter 12 The Keys 70
Chapter 13 The Main Factor 77
Chapter 14 Living in His Light 85

Prayer 94
Resources Page 97
Biblical Declarations 100
Acknowledgments 102
Notes 106

Introduction

Welcome to Speak Submit Surrender, a story of God's faithfulness and how He led me to overcome a difficult season in my life. Thank you for taking this journey along with me. How vital it is for us to speak and to share how we overcame! Yes, it is key to use our voices as a weapon of transformation even beyond resistance, especially as women! I used to avoid sharing my story. Looking back now, telling my story was needed and still is needed. Through all the pain, God showed me it was necessary to share my story with others because my story helps contribute to my sisters' growth and healing journey and vice versa. Sharing our stories is needed to help empower and equip others through their life's journey! The purpose of my story is to point others to the Light in the midst of darkness. No matter how much we are tempted to run from our past and what we went through, it is still a part of our testimony! And no shame or fear should hold us back from sharing our stories. Our stories can be used as a weapon to overcome the darkness in this world (see Revelation 12:11a).

God created each and every one of us to be unique and special. Think about your fingerprints. Each one of them is so distinctly different. If you take a look closer at your finger, you will see the annular rings that sit closely together to make up your unique fingerprint. Even the fingerprints on each finger are discrete. Have you tried to unlock your phone with your index finger instead of your thumb? Just like our fingerprints, we were all created by God with the intentionality to be uniquely distinct. We were created for a divine purpose to display God's glory on Earth!

Maybe you're probably saying, "yeah, but not me," or "I wasn't even supposed to be here." But guess what, God created you on purpose! In the book of Jeremiah, God says, "I knew you before I formed you in your mother's womb" (Jeremiah 1:5a NLT), meaning He knew us and had a purpose for us before our mothers and our fathers have even conceived us. We never were an afterthought in God's eyes. Everything from our names to the number of hair on our head, God knows about (Luke 12:7 NLT)!

No matter what we go through in life, God's grace is more powerful than our pains! God never promised a perfect life, but He did promise that in Jesus Christ we will overcome (1 John 4:4). For me personally, when I began to draw closer and abide in God, I became bold and more whole as a person. By God's love, grace, and mercy, I did not let the heartache of pain and hardship ruin my life! The beautiful part of encountering God is that He chose us first, He chose us to commune and to live in His presence! What a beautiful privilege and an honor! And from there, we can begin a wondrous journey with Him!

Never let anything hold you back from evolving, growing, and becoming the powerful woman you were called to be before the foundations of time! You were created to be uniquely you! You were called to arise and shine for such a time as time! Your lovely presence fills every environment you walk into! Who you are, your voice, your story, how you overcame is needed on the earth!

I wrote this book in a narrative and reflective style of writing. Reflecting can be a beautiful thing. I saw a quote on Pinterest that said, "Maybe God invites us to remember, not to torment us but to teach us." That quote helps me change my perspective on sharing my testimony and not running away from my story.

Throughout the first few chapters, I will be unpacking the time of how I survived an abusive relationship. Then I will discuss how I overcame trauma, and how I began to thrive and flourish! I will also share how God led me through an escape plan that removed me from the toxic relationship I was in. This escape plan includes three particular parts. First, I had to speak. Secondly, I had to submit. Finally, I chose to surrender. Through God's grace, He walked me through this plan and strengthened me to do all three steps. God also taught me how to interact with Him as the triune God (God the Father, God the Son, and God the Spirit) by speaking, submitting, and surrendering unto Him. I will discuss more of this throughout the book.

In addition to that, God led me to amazing resources that helped me tremendously throughout this journey. There is a list of resources listed at the end of the book. As we journey through the second and third sections of this book, I will be discussing pivotal moments I had with God to maintain the good work He started within me. What was meant for evil, God can turn it around for the good (Genesis 50:20)! Thank you, God! And guess what? God doesn't have any favorites; He can and wants to do the same for you in your life!

This book will give you tools and strategies on how you can overcome whatever may be entrapping you! Use my story as a prototype to see the ways and techniques of how you can overcome whatever may be holding you back in your life (whether it's hopelessness, fear, comparison, etc.). My story is one of an overcomer to another overcomer! I pray you will be empowered to be bold and take the audacious steps to walk in the identity and destiny God created for you!

Section I

Chapter 1

Dark Days in December

I went through his phone then all hell broke loose...

A couple of years ago, in December, it was one of the darkest days of my life! I knew everything wasn't perfect, but this was the person I wanted to be with. Gregory and I had been together for a while now, and I loved him. I was creating the perfect family image I've always wanted, even if it meant ignoring certain things that were happening that I knew was wrong. *If I have to silence myself for my dream of having the perfect family, then so be it*, is what I thought. But that day in December was different. I was tired. I was emotionally done. I reached the end of myself trying to force something that wasn't there. This was the final straw. This was the straw that broke the camel's back.

Being in a toxic relationship is so dangerous. All of those destructive behaviors can become a lifestyle. All of the cursings, manipulating, throwing things, yelling, and so on became a norm. Living a life filled with cycles of sin and toxicity took a toll on me, mentally as well as physically. A couple of months before that dark day in December, I began to get sharp chest pains; the nurses could not find the reason for them. But I knew what caused it. It was stress.

I just didn't want to admit it. Not only I was a recipient of the toxic behaviors, but I displayed them as well. The worst part was when the toxicity became our new normal within the relationship. This toxic relationship with my ex-boyfriend, Gregory, was my new normal. My physical health took a toll for the worst as a result of my life at the time.

In a way, I felt stuck in life. I was dealing with so much externally and internally. I began to feel overwhelmed. It was a lot going on at once. I was in a place where I wasn't completely happy, but I wasn't sad. I was numb. I was complacent. I didn't want to break up with Gregory because I didn't want to become a single mother again. I knew there is nothing wrong with being a single mom. I grew up around strong single mothers. I just thought that I couldn't be that strong to raise a child on my own. Plus, I idolized sex, marriage, and having a family. My idolatry for sex and marriage led me to compromise. (An idol is a person, place, thing, or feeling one honors more than Jesus). So I stayed in the relationship. *Plus, it wasn't bad all the time*, I would often think. I can tell you this: when it got bad, it got really bad!

It was only three days before Christmas, and I was ready to celebrate the holiday. I was planning to go to church that Christmas morning. I was looking forward to the holiday season. I was also looking forward to the new chapter of my life. In addition to that, I was super excited to put some money down for our spring wedding. It was the first deposit for the venue we checked out a couple of months before! The wedding was less than five months away. Even though I didn't feel any peace about getting married, I was looking forward to it. I have dreamt of getting married since I was a little girl. *This is the right thing to do, Kim,* I told myself. And, to me, at the time, it was the right thing to do. I looked past all of those red flags both Gregory and I displayed throughout our relationship. I continued to suppress my concerns and decided to move forward with getting married. Plus, I felt like my life and my soul was intertwined with Gregory at the time. We had sex before our planned wedding day that led us to create a deep bond with one another, a soul-tie—so getting married made sense. Months later, into the relationship, I started to feel guilty about having sex outside of marriage.

Even though I had been having sex for years, I began to feel different for about the past two months. I had these horrible feelings immediately afterward; I started to feel convicted about it. So I decided to be celibate within my sexually active relationship, but I didn't respect that decision for too long. *It will be easy just to stop*, so I thought, but I was very wrong. I began thinking about that bible verse, 'it is better to marry than to burn with lust' (1 Corinthians 7:9). So I thought, *why don't we hurry up and get married. I love you, and you love me, why not?* Bad idea! I began to experience what happens when one neglects God along with godly counsel and tries to control their own life. I saw how disastrous it was to try to sprinkle a bible verse over a hot mess of a situation. That was not a great idea at all. Extremely stubborn and naive, I continued to ignore the red flags in our relationship.

Back to that dark day in December. Let me tell you; it went from bad to worse. It was a calm Tuesday evening; I went through his phone then all hell broke loose. I saw something I didn't want to see, and I immediately felt that my trust in him was betrayed. I confronted Gregory about it, and an argument turned into an intense moment where cops were called. In no way, shape, or form, I thought going through Gregory's phone would lead to cops asking me what felt like was a million questions. I didn't know that confronting an issue would lead me to see my phone slammed against the royal blue colored wall. Once I saw that phone hit that blue wall and split into two, I immediately thought, *it's time for me to take my son and get up out of here.*

As he left the room, I thought I would get my son in his clothes and leave for my neighbor's place, but I didn't make it out the door at that moment. As I quietly put on my son's clothes, I heard Gregory talking to my relative, Valerie, on the phone. I heard him telling his side of the story and that I was crazy. I had no phone. Even though

I had no way of defending myself, I still had my voice. I screamed at the top of my lungs. I never screamed like that in my life. But I guess you will do whatever you need to do to survive in a time of survival. He threw his phone to the side and pushed me against the wall while balling up his hand, pulling back his arm to punch me in the face. All while I was holding my child in my hands. He quickly changed his mind, took a few steps back, yelled, and threw my purse across the room. Then he took the car keys and walked out of the door. I truly do believe that it was no one but Jesus Christ who saved me at that very moment!

I had nothing to call the police with, but immediately I saw my laptop. I knew I might not have too much time, so I opened my computer, went on social media, and messaged my friend, Sarah, to call the cops. I quickly sent the message to her. As I heard the doorknob moving, I quickly closed the laptop and put it away. Gregory walked through the door, and right behind him was Valerie, whom he called a couple of minutes earlier. All the fear I had inside of me began to leave as the feeling of anger arose and replaced it. Just hearing Valerie, my own family member, immediately take up Gregory's side was beyond frustrating. Gregory was surprisingly very calm, and they BOTH were telling me to calm down as if I was crazy. Now looking back, I can see that they were gaslighting me. I was so angry. I began to pace and yell at both of them. This all happened within a few minutes after sending that message to Sarah.

Chapter 2

Face to Face

A few minutes later, the two police officers walked through the door. One police officer talked to Gregory while the other spoke to me. I was so upset. I felt like I was going crazy, I thought the only way not to seem crazy was to be silent. I tried my best to calm myself down as much as possible and told the officer what happened.

My leg was shaking as I spoke. I was taking slow and steady breaths between my words, trying to calm myself down. Then I asked the officer if he could take my son and I to a safe location. He looked at me with a stern look and told me, "NO." He said he wasn't allowed to take us and that we would have to find our own way out. I was shocked as they continued explaining their protocol.

My friend, Sarah, quickly came over. She stood beside the cop as he continued to talk about protocol and how he couldn't give us a ride anywhere. I felt like I was losing my mind. My life felt like I was in that old show, The Twilight Zone. *This can't be my life*, I thought. After the cops left, I carried my son to my room, Sarah followed us. She asked about my phone, I told her what happened and how it broke. She looked behind the furniture to find the pieces of the phone. To my surprise, it didn't break, but the battery popped out. When Sarah put the battery back in the phone, it worked again! She handed me the phone, and at that moment I didn't know who to call. Who would I call in this type of situation? I felt like I was at a dead end. So, I called my local police district, and they told me the same thing the cops told me. I felt so hurt, angry, scared, and confused about what to do next. I also felt hopeless. But God gave me the power and strength to keep going, to survive this situation…

Sometimes we don't think about how much effort it takes for us to speak! Growing up, I never had the vocabulary for who I was, how I was created, or where I wanted to be in life. I passively went along with the flow of life and everything it threw at me. But now, looking back, I realized that I wasn't the average girl. I was very quiet, and I could easily dismiss everyone in the classroom. It may sound like I was an introvert but let me tell you this, it was more than that. I created a whole world, which was very far from the real world. I lived in a place of isolation. Little did I know that God created me like this so that I would occasionally experience times of solitude with Him. My mind was my secret place, and my sin patterns were my comfort zone. It was very dysfunctional. Plus, it didn't help that life wasn't easy for me growing up. Pain, trauma, and abuse all played a part in my childhood. So when I disassociated myself from the realities of life, I felt safe.

I continued to have this mindset into adulthood. I found myself living in my daydreams more than my reality. They kept me ignorant of the worries of life. At the time, this world I created to be in my head was my safe haven, I had to work through a lot of trust issues to be more transparent. Even now, I am continuously learning to be transparent with those private areas in my heart with God, myself, and with others. Earlier I said my mind was a secret place, but those toxic and damaging thought patterns didn't remain there. All of it started to show up in my life in one way or another. I saw myself expressing and tolerating those toxic patterns. I began to see myself living out the traumas I survived from childhood.

As an adult, I became more and more silent about my own feelings and emotions. I suppressed most of my emotions because of fear. I carried that belief into my relationships. Fear began to show up within my relationships in a way that I felt like things weren't right and I chose not saying anything about it or I justified it. *At least the situation isn't that bad*, I would say to myself. Unintentionally, I began to gaslight myself while silencing my own voice. What do I mean by my voice? I mean the confidence and the boldness to say what I needed to say and mean what I say regardless of fear and anxiety. Without my voice, I was in danger.

In the midst of everything that was happening during those dark days in December, I found myself so indecisive. Should I go this way or that way? Should I take this route or that one? Should I try to reconcile Gregory or should I not? I felt like I was going crazy. I needed to look past my wants and acknowledge what my needs are! And I needed to do this fast! My future was depending on it.

Although my wants consisted of going back into the relationship I had with Gregory, trying to confront the toxic and abusive behaviors we had, and continuing to plan our scheduled wedding, my needs screamed inside of me "GET OUT" and "I. DON'T. FEEL. SAFE."! Looking back, I can remember suppressing my needs throughout our relationship and even throughout my life. I became codependent. Looking back, I am so grateful God showed me this techniques of clearly re-evaluating my wants vs. my needs, counting the cost, and using my voice and actions to affirm healthy decisions and boundaries.

After calling the police distinct, I felt stuck. Not only stuck physically but stuck emotionally. I stayed in my room at the moment to figure out what's next. I never thought my relationship with Gregory would've ended up as an abusive domestic situation. To be honest, our relationship was abusive the whole time. We both was showing signs of abuse. I couldn't run from that fact anymore; I had to come face to face with what was happening. All the signs were there. Domestic abuse can be apparent or subtle.

There are different types of abuse, including physical, emotional, financial, etc. Signals of abuse can include isolating one from their family or friends, manipulating one with words to influence their decision-making, abusing one's body and property, hitting, pushing, and even excessive criticizing. Other signs can also include belittling, name-calling, gaslighting, neglecting to discuss problematic and toxic behaviors, aggressiveness, violating one's personal space, and more. If you are in an abusive and toxic relationship of any kind, seek help immediately. For more information about domestic violence and different signs of it, visit www.thehotline.org.

Moments later (after calling the police district), I sat in the side of my bed, distraught. I didn't know who to call next. I needed a way out. I feel so stuck, physically and emotionally. Fear, sadness, and anger were gripping me all at once; I didn't know what to do next. God led me to call my friend from college, Janah. I thought *if she picks up the phone maybe she could let me and my son stay with her, it's perfect place because no one knows where she leaves, we'll be safe.* Anxiety increased with every ring as I was on the other line, hoping Janah would pick up the phone. She answered the phone! "Hello" she said, with a curious tone in her voice. It was almost 11 o'clock at night. "Hi Janah, It's Kim", I answered.

I continued to tell her about every that happened that night, everything from the argument to the police. I told her that I didn't feel safe and I was looking for a place to stay for a bit until I got my life together somehow. She sincerely invited my son and me to stay with her. I thanked her and told her that we will be there that night. We hung up the phone, and I began to pack some clothes for us to leave. Later that night, after Sarah left, we arrived at Janah's place.

Chapter 3

Crisis At Hand

*Y*ears later, I could look back and can say that I was in a major crisis. That crisis was an identity crisis. There were many factors that showed me I was unprepared for a relationship at that time. Those factors included: not knowing who I was, not honoring and loving how God created me to be, not acknowledging specific standards I need to place in my life in order to thrive, not respecting my own and others' boundaries, and more.

As I continue to reflect, it was important for me to acknowledge some of these factors to implement the lessons into my life now without going into self-blame. I am not responsible for other people's actions. You are not responsible for other people's actions. We each are only responsible for our own actions towards others and towards ourselves. It is pivotal to show ourselves self-compassion throughout our life journey while also sincerely turning away (or repenting) from the wrongs we have done in God's eyes.

Looking back and seeing that I had an identity crisis was major to me in so many ways. Not knowing who we are at any time in our lives is a crisis for us and everyone connected to us. By not knowing who we are, we can risk throwing away our future God had intended for us. We may depend on our own understanding and limited mind state if we move outside our God-given identity. We may even begin to compare ourselves to others to create a false sense of identity for ourselves. By not knowing who God created us to be, we can end up going in circles within our relationships, friendships, careers, and even habits that lead us to live a compromised life while hindering us from reaching our God-given destiny. I pray even as you are reading this right now that God, according to His love and mercy (Psalm 103:8), will begin to speak to you about your identity. I pray He will give you insight on how and why He created you, in Jesus name! You are perfectly created in the image of God, and He loves you beyond your understanding.

See, here's the thing! God is multifaceted! God is gracious, and He is merciful, He is also loving, caring, kind, just, and so much more. And since God made us in His image through Jesus Christ (Genesis 1:27, John 1:3), we are also multifaceted. There is so much more to us than the natural eye can see! There is so much more of you than what you can see right now! When I looked up the word *multifaceted*, it is defined as "having many different parts or sides" (Cambridge University Press 2021). Another definition of the word is compared to the concept of a gem, like a diamond or a ruby. Rubies are very much multifaceted. Rubies are rare and expensive gemstones, usually displayed in the color of blood-red. The price of rubies can range anywhere from $2,000 to 1 million dollars per carat. They are found in the countries of Myanmar, Thailand, and Sri Lanka (Britannica 2020). There are many different types of rubies, and each of them can display a different shape, size, and even color in a particular environment. I don't think we fully can understand the beauty and the complexity of rubies unless we have studied or even mine them ourselves.

Just like rubies, there is so much more to us than meets the eye. There is so much more of you and me than what we can see now! Never settle for the limited comprehension of what you know now. Go deeper! Dive into the presence of God by praying, fasting, repenting, praising and thanking Him, reading His Holy Scriptures: The Bible, and more. Go deeper with God in the however way His Spirit is leading you. Build and expand your relationship with Him. Ask God to reveal a part of you that He created through His Son, Jesus Christ.

This is also something that God has been showing me. He has saved me from that mindset and showed me to place my identity to Who is eternal, which is Him. Through His Divine Son, Jesus Christ, He describes Himself the Alpha and the Omega, the Beginning and the End (Revelation 22:13 NLT) because Jesus is the meaning of forever. When this world is over or when we come to the end of our days, God will be there to lovingly embrace us into His presence if we place our trust in His Holy Son, Jesus Christ, here on this earth! Once we enter into accepting Jesus Christ as our Lord and Savior, by the grace of God, there we will find our true identity!

Finding our identity outside of God in temporary things can feel like a never-ending roller-coaster. Finding our identity is the key to many different areas of our lives. It gives us security and fulfillment by embracing our true identity that was placed inside of us before the foundation of this world was even created. That's why so many of us can get lost in finding our identity. But what if I told you this? What if I told you there is one person that truly knows our identity, that one person is God! Because our identity is in Him! Our true identity is rooted in being a child of God through the salvation of Jesus Christ. This is something I wished I would've known before dating. Instead of trying to solidify my identity within a relationship with another person, God just wanted me to solidify my relationship first with Him.

God created each and every one of us in such a distinct and unique way that our innermost beings yearn for Him. Sometimes we indulge in other things, such as food, sex, drugs, gambling, technology, and work to give us a type of fulfillment that only God can give. In Psalm 139, the writer wrote these beautiful words, "I will praise You, for I am fearfully and wonderfully made..." (Psalm 139:

14a NKJV). The writer was praising God, and he knew he was fearfully and wonderfully made. I like to use the dictionary as I study different words to help me understand the sentence better. Let's look up the words, fearfully and wonderfully! In the dictionary, fearfully means "full of awe." In context within this bible verse being fearfully created means, God created us with awe and respect. Wonderfully means "of excellence, amazement, greatness." Bringing all of those words together in Psalm 139 verse 14, says how God made you with awe, respect, excellence, and amazement!

Have you ever gone to a painting or pottery class and were amazed at what you created by the end of the class? You put so much time and effort you put into your creation! Attentively going through the process, you know that every detail matters! Your creation can take you minutes, hours, or even days to make. But in the end, you've created a masterpiece before you. Take that feeling and times it by more than one billion! That's how God felt when He created you!

This verse is Psalm 139 is commonly used for some of us that we may become familiar with it. For some of us who have already heard that bible verse so often, maybe God is trying to reveal something new this time! Let us not get so familiar with Scripture that we miss what God's Holy Spirit is trying to communicate to us. Let us move away from a place of familiarity and approach Scripture from a place of humility. To view the Bible as our guide and teacher, we are God's students, quietly listening, asking questions, and getting ready to learn, listen, and/or getting redirected by God's Holy Spirit through His precious Word.

For other of us, maybe we have never heard of this Scripture verse before. This is an invitation to begin to get your Bible (or Bible app) and let God speak through His Beautiful Word to you. I spent years reading the Bible, but something began to change when I gave my life to Jesus Christ by faith, and I started to speak to God as my Heavenly Father and build my relationship with Him through the leading of His Holy Spirit. Later in my journey with

God, He instructed me to speak His truth in His Word (The Bible) over myself. Not in a manipulative way or trying to force or manifest my own will over my life, but in a way that is holy and pleasing unto God.

With the leading of Holy Spirit, I searched the Scriptures to understand God's will over my life and began to speak that. You're probably asking, *What do you mean, Kim?* I mean the Scripture, by the grace and Spirit of God, became my source of empowerment. I began to realize that my words are a tool to help build myself. I began to pray the Word of God over myself, clinging on to faith and the powerful weight of God's Holy Word. I began to speak biblical declarations over myself.

Years later, in the month of December. I heard God declaratively say in my heart: open up your mouth! That was my call to take action, to wake up, to stop letting life and the devil have their way with me. This was my wake-up call to stop being passive! I obeyed the voice of God, repented for all of my sins, and I began to speak to God as my Heavenly Father and speak His words over myself! I said, *I was fearfully and wonderfully made by Papa God according to Psalm 139, in Jesus mighty name!* I'll be honest, when I began to speak to God as my Father about what was truly in my heart and to speak His word over myself, I felt silly. I had thoughts that said *this is stupid, I should stop.* That was the enemy, in the form of self-sabotage, trying to prevent me from speaking God's Word and to keep me from building up my faith!

Even the Word of God calls us to walk by faith and not by what we see (Hebrews 10:38). I kept going. I wasn't consistent in prayer and saying the biblical declarations every day, but I kept going! And by the grace of God, I didn't give up! Now I wish I can tell you I saw a change within that day, but I didn't. I wish I can tell you I saw a change within that week, but I didn't. Even though I did not see instant changes, God began to transform me from the inside out. God taught me how to preserve in prayer and how to uproot toxic and demonic seeds and plant good, Godly biblical seeds in my mind and in my heart with His Holy Word.

> Your words are so powerful that they will kill or give life…
> —Proverbs 18:21a TPT

There is power in the words we speak! Begin to speak to God, honestly, openly and authentically. And begin to speak His Word over yourself, that's why this section is entitled: SPEAK! Say it with me, *God created me; I was fearfully and wonderfully made!* Yass! Say it again! No more being careless and reckless with our words! No more putting ourselves in environments where others are allowed to speak to us any type of way, calling us out of our name, etc. No more! It is time to speak God's truth over us! Let us not get use to saying only negative and depressive statements. It's time for us to seek God and to speak His Word! It is time for us to see ourselves how God sees us and to see others how God sees them! It is time for us to seek our identity in God's presence!

We need to leave all of the old and toxic thought patterns about ourselves behind and search for something new. When you are after God and His perfect will for your life, and He is ordering your steps, it is all worth it! Don't let your trust issues stand in the way of what God has in store for you! One bible verse put it like this, "Eyes have not seen, nor have ears heard, nor have entered into the heart of man the things which God has prepared for those who love Him" (1 Corinthians 2:9 NKJV). Believing this truth has reassured me of my identity in God and influenced my expectations within relationships and more.

Chapter 4

Unmuzzled

A few years ago, I began to ask God some honest questions: who am I? Who have You created me to be? And before He began to talk to me about my identity, I had first to let go and surrender all of the things I thought I was. I had to submit to this new way of living, a way that walked closely with God.

It was only by God's grace that He led me closer to Him. He guides me on how to seek Him first. The abundance of God's grace and mercy that He gives us to turn from our sins and sinful nature by repenting and believing in the death, burial, and resurrection of Jesus Christ! For that, I want to say glory be to God! It's only by His grace and mercy that I can write these things to you.

> So let us come boldly to the throne of our gracious God. There we will receive his mercy, and we will find grace to help us when we need it most.
>
> —Hebrews 4:16 NLT

Sidenote: I know the term 'mercy and grace' may have been thrown around a lot, especially if we grew up in the church. But let's break down each word for a deeper understanding. This is an excellent reminder for me to remind my soul of the very foundation of our faith. In the Merriam-Webster dictionary, Grace is defined as undeserved divine assistance given to humans for their spiritual rebirth or transformation. Another definition of grace is approval or favor. As for mercy, it is described as compassion in the Merriam-Webster dictionary. (To do an in-depth study of the words 'mercy and grace' in this bible verse, we should dive into the original Hebrew or Greek meaning; there are amazing resources available to us, such as biblehub.com, that can help us do that). By receiving God's compassion and undeserved assistance/favor, we can encounter His presence in new ways!

Once we confess with our mouth that Jesus is Lord and believe in our heart that God has Him from the dead, we are saved and receive the saving grace of God (also known as salvation – see Romans 10:9). We begin the process of dying to our sinful desires and looking more like Jesus Christ each day (also known as the sanctification). Sanctification is the process of being transformed, through the power of the Holy Spirit, to look more like Jesus Christ. Sanctification is a transformative process that leads all of us to help us reflect Jesus' name and nature on the earth.

Once God began to reveal parts of who He created me to be, some things started to finally make sense. For instance, He showed me that I was passive. I was taking life as it was dished to me without resisting, without even praying. Other things about myself, I still don't understand. I would ask God questions like, *Why me? Why did you call me to do this?* For example, when God put it in my heart to write a book, I became nervous, excited, and anxious all at the same time. But I began to question God, saying in my heart *Why me?* and *Why now?'* In Psalm 55, verse 22, the writer instructs us to cast our cares on the Lord, and He will sustain you; He will never let the righteous be shaken. And even in Isaiah 55 verse 8 (NKJV), the Word of God says, "For My thoughts *are* not your thoughts, Nor *are* your ways My ways," says the LORD." Wow! Even in the midst of uncertainty and doubt, God still encourages us to turn to Him and trust in His supreme power. He invites us to leave our troubles on Him through prayer because He is a loving and patient Father to those who trust in Jesus Christ.

Prayer is important. Prayer is essential, especially now-a-days. Through prayer is where I find perfect peace! In the presence of God, there is fullness of joy (Psalm 16:11b). Sometimes I find hope when I remember how powerful God is. And through His love, He leads me not to ask *why* but to ask, *how*? *God, show me HOW I can obey You!* My heart's cry was *"God show me how I can speak to you as a Heavenly Father and your Word over my life"*. God led me to ask how, instead of why. After I ask how, He began to show me how to commune with Him as His child. He taught me to speak to Him from a sincere heart like a child, instead of just praying from a place of routine or tradition. He showed me that speaking to Him required honesty and honor, and not perfection. He offered me the beautiful gift of repentance. He silenced the voice of fear (2 Timothy 1:7 NLT). He also taught me how to boldly pray through His Word by His will and not my own.

In Isaiah 55, God says, "My thoughts are nothing like your thoughts," says the LORD. "And my ways are far beyond anything you could imagine" (Isaiah 55:8 NLT). Understanding every decision and move of God is something, we, as humans, will never be able to do. But we can always choose to trust Him and have faith in Him. We can choose to pray unto God and ask for His guidance and peace. We can give Him our praise and thanksgiving for being an Almighty God! We can repent and turn away from our wicked ways. We can receive His forgiveness and give Him our burdens. As loving and caring as He is, God welcomes all of these things and more through His lovingkindness and His mercy!

God gave us a beautiful invitation to commune with Him when He sent His only anointed Son, Jesus Christ, to Earth to do and fulfill His holy will. Jesus taught and spoke so much about prayer and communing with God. Not only did Jesus spoke about prayer, but He also demonstrated a lifestyle of prayer as He occasionally secluded Himself to commune with God (see Luke 5:16). In the Bible (specifically within the Books of Matthew, Mark, Luke, and John), we see many accounts where Jesus left groups and even His disciples to pray and speak to God. Ultimately, Jesus is the One who gives us the grace, ability, and the blueprint on how to speak and pray unto God (Luke 11).

As I mentioned earlier, God showed me how I was passive and muzzled. I didn't understand that I had the power to turn my life around, I had the authority to do it through Christ Jesus. I was so silenced that I would even subconsciously place my hand over my mouth when I was feeling anxious. But something happened after that tough season in my life. God taught me to open up my mouth and to pray unto Him as my Heavenly Father. He taught me to speak His Word over my life. He taught me how to prophesy Jesus' heart over my life and my child's life. He also taught me how to follow the leading of His Holy Spirit and to repent from the sins that held me back from building a relationship with Him. I even grew in the areas of contentment and holy expectation because of God. I saw myself growing into a better and more gracious woman, mother, daughter, friend because of Him.

God is so faithful; even in our unfaithfulness, He still speaks, teaches, and ministers to us. God kindly showed me my identity. He sent new friends and mentors to reaffirm how God sees me. God use these relationships and healthy biblical community to help sharpen each of us look more like Jesus Christ in our everyday lives. He taught me many things about myself, His kingdom, His Word, His heart, and so much more! He showed me that I am loved (Jeremiah 31:3 NKJV). He chose me, and I am a part of a royal priesthood (1 Peter 2:9 NLT). In God's presence, you can find your identity and the Lover of your Soul, Jesus Christ. Jesus is the One who affirms you! Jesus is the One who sees you! Jesus is the One who hears you!

One of the many tools God led me to use to contribute to my journey of escaping toxic relationships and behaviors is biblical declarations. Biblical declarations are declarative statements that derive from the Bible. Biblical declarations can be used as an empowering tool to help build one's faith and esteem in God. It is so pivotal to declare Jesus' heart over your life. He gave me His words to speak over myself and empowering words to speak over others. By speaking God's words, it felt like God removed a muzzle that was over my mouth and gave me the courage to me to speak!

Not only we can read what God's word says about us, but we can also boldly speak God's word over us! As women, we are called to be gentle but not timid. Time is up for timidness and insecurity! Don't let others or yourself speak anything opposite to God's perfect will and hope for you and your life! Open up your mouth and SPEAK over yourself. There is a time and place to speak the Word of God over your life! The time is now! Let us not delay any longer! No more passivity, in Jesus name! May we have the wisdom to speak when God tells us to speak, and may we be quiet when God tells us to be quiet, in Jesus name! If God is for us, who can ever be against us? (Romans 8:31b). At this time, let us open up our mouths and speak God's words!

Here are some bold declarations that encouraged me throughout my walk with God, especially during the tough times of my life:

> I was made through the image of God
> (GENESIS 1:27)
>
> I can do anything through Christ who strengthens me
> (PHILIPPIANS 4:13)
>
> I am a child of God and I am called for such a time as time
> (GALATIANS 3:26, ESTHER 4:14B, 1 PETER 2:9)
>
> No weapons formed against my family and I shall prosper
> (ISAIAH 54:17A)

> God lives within me; I will not fall
> (Psalm 46:5)

> Do not be afraid or discouraged, for the Lord will personally go ahead of me. He will be with me; He will neither fail me nor abandon me
> (Deuteronomy 31:8)

And I declare those statement not in my power or authority, but in the power, authority, and name of Jesus Christ! There are some more of these biblical declarations in towards the end of this book. You may be feeling tired and weary right now but keep going! Jesus is rooting for you! I am rooting for you! Keep going! Keep writing down those powerful words and speak them over yourself! As a child of God, and through the name and salvation of Jesus Christ, you can claim your rights that are written in God's Holy Word! God wants to unmuzzle you and me to proclaim and testify of His goodness! Continue to speak over yourself, your family, your community, your city, your nation! Speak hope! Speak joy! Speak peace! Speak love! You might not see the fruits of your words now, but don't get discouraged! Keep planting those Godly seeds, and the harvest will soon come (Galatians 6:9)! Also, speak about what you may be going through with others, whether it's trusted family members, friends, therapists, coaches, leaders, spiritual counselors, etc. Whether you are in the middle of your dark days or you are in the midst of your joyous ones, know that God is with you! You are not alone! We are cheering for you to be victorious in Christ Jesus! Survive what you're going through, begin to thrive, and then FLOURISH in Christ Jesus through His lovingkindness and goodness for His glory alone!

Section II

Submit

Chapter 5

The Escape Plan

An "escape plan" is usually described as a plan to escape an adverse situation, environment, or circumstance, whether it's a relationship, a prison, a burning building, etc. While observing different parts of our lives, we may see cycles of bad patterns or situations. Sometimes we are caught in the same cycle for so long that we may become numb to the toxic situation. We can ask God for insight and wisdom see our situations how He sees them. We can also ask Him to help us develop an escape plan for any toxic situation in our lives, whether it's in relationships, finances, within ourselves, etc. The Bible says that God will generously give wisdom to those who ask and do not doubt (James 1:5-6). God is so brilliant that He is able to give us His divine wisdom to help us escape those adverse situations that we may be in!

Looking back, I can see it was my whole life that was toxic, but especially in the area of my emotional state of mind. During those tough seasons in my life, I felt so stuck. I didn't have a plan. Some people say that every person in a toxic and abusive relationship should have an escape plan if things get out of control. Escape plans in a domestic abusive situation may include keeping extra bags of clothes in the truck of your car in case if you need to leave with your children suddenly. Other escape plans may include having a charged pre-paid phone hidden in one's home, some extra cash, a list of safe places one can go to if the situation worsens, etc. (If you or someone you know is in any type of danger, please seek help immediately).

Even though I didn't have an escape plan, I thank God for Janah, my friend from college, who picked up the phone that night and invited us to stay with her. Looking back, Janah was the perfect person to stay with because no one knew where she lived, including me. My place was too much of a toxic environment for my son and I to spend the night there. We needed to leave ASAP. I knew that if I stayed, things would've gotten worse!

When we arrived at Janah's place, she quietly hugged me and gave us some bedsheets to sleep on her bed as she slept on the floor. I am filled with gratitude for a friend who was willing to risk their own safety to help us in our time of need. The next day I called out of work. I spent the next few days figuring out what I should do next. The fact I woke up in Janah's place made everything so surreal to me. I couldn't run away from this reality. Even though I knew what I need to do. I still wanted to work things out with my ex at the time.

Morning turned into nights, and nights turn into days. One afternoon, Janah looked at me and asked me what am I going to do. *I had to do something, we can't stay here forever,* I thought. I was internally trying to avoid my reality. I didn't want to be a single mother again, so I catered to my wants instead of paying attention to my need. My needs included being courageous, placing healthy boundaries for myself, and being determined to live a peaceful life in Christ Jesus. My needs also included forgiving Gregory fully and freely while not tolerating abusive behaviors from him, others, or myself. In the words of author Tony A. Gaskins Jr., "loving yourself may mean walking away." By setting and respecting certain boundaries, I begin to display healthy love and respect for myself. Over these past few years, I learned that although God instructs us to love our enemies (Matthew 5:44), He doesn't want us to be in dangerous relationships and environments (Proverbs 4:23, Proverbs 22:3). And God has a true definition of what love is. We will discuss later in Chapter 13: The Main Factor.

On the other side of that spectrum, my wants were hoping to work things out with Gregory, even after everything that just happen. *My dream of getting married was depended on it,* my heart cried. I was holding on tight to the fear of being alone and the idolatry of marriage. I was committed to the old without considering the new possibilities. What thought, idea, mindset, or idol that is leading you to hold on to something that does not benefit you or your future?

I talked to Gregory a few days later, asking him if we can work things out, maybe we can go to therapy together. He said no. After a few days of staying with Janah, I thank her for everything, packed up our stuff, and returned to my place after speaking to Gregory, ensuring that he moved out. I was filled with hurt, bitterness, vindictiveness, and sorrow. That whole season in my life taught me a vital lesson to pay attention to my needs instead of my wants and simply move on. Looking back, I thank God for that no, and I learned that I shouldn't base my personal decisions on my own emotions, idols, or even other people's opinions. Instead, my personal decisions should in what God tells me to do and submit to His plans. That *no* protected both Gregory and me from re-entering the toxic relationship we once had. I heard a saying in a Youtube video by author and preacher Kimberly Jones, also known as Real Talk Kim. In this video, she said that *rejection is God's protection*. I completely agree!

Later that week, a church I used to attend in college called Epiphany Fellowship, had service that Christmas Sunday. On that day, one of the church pastors, Pastor Curtis Dunlap, began to preach. The sermon was entitled *Down But Not Out,* based on the Book of Genesis, Chapter 3. As Pastor Curtis was preaching, my mind felt like it was running 100 miles per hour; it was so hard to remain focused during the sermon. I was tired of running, tired of fighting, and to be honest, tired of living. Towards the end of the sermon, Pastor Dunlap said some things that caught my attention.

Before Pastor Dunlap ending the sermon, I heard him say *'No matter how bad it may look in your life, it's not over until God says it's over.'* Then a few seconds later, he said, *'…when God shows up, you have to remember that even though you may be harmed, you haven't been defeated'*. Streams of tears fell down my face and onto my blue dress as I held my son in my hands. It's like God was talking directly to me. Although I felt like a constant disappointment to God, it didn't stop Him from encouraging me and loving me during those dark days. God's love and grace rescued me and empowered me to keep going!

Immediately that heaviness on my heart began to lift. Thoughts of suicide began to leave. I felt refreshed and recharged by God! I was determined to move on emotionally and to leave that abusive relationship I had with myself. I was determined to live the peaceful life I've always imagined for myself and my child. I repented to God for my sins and began to live for God by His grace! I truly thank God for leading me to Epiphany Fellowship church and for Pastor Dunlap's sermon that Christmas Sunday!

> But if we own up to our sins, God shows that He is faithful and just by forgiving us of our sins and purifying us from the pollution of all the bad things we have done.
> —1 John 1:9 (Voice)

To this day, I am truly overwhelmed with gratitude that God led me out of those toxic relationships. I don't take that lightly. I thank God for His mercy, kindness, and grace! Months later, God continued to give me wisdom, insight, different strategies, and resources to protect my child and me, staying out of abusive relationships, and so much more!

God delivered and counseled me. He wanted to heal my soul, but first, He wanted me to repent and release the hurt, the shame, the fears, and more. The next couple of years were an intense deliverance and healing process that God brought me through. This process showed me my past, where I was broken, and the beautiful journey of healing in Jesus Christ. This process also led me to an amazing church, biblical community, excellent books, phenomenal counselors, virtual groups and so much more. My unique escape plan was to undergo these three vital steps of speaking, submitting, and surrendering unto God. Submitting myself to Jesus Christ, His saving grace, His lordship, and His divine plans has helped me endure the difficult season in my life!

I pray if you are reading (or listening) to this and if you are in a toxic situation, that by the grace and mercy of God, He will deliver and heal you; and that He will generously give you your unique escape plan. I pray that He will lead you to Himself and all types of resources so that you can come out of the adverse situation in freedom and victoriously in Jesus mighty name! Let us not allow other people's words or actions to lead us to feel less than who God created us to be. Let us not allow even our own words and/or actions hold us back from being the person God called us to be. Let's repent and release everything unto God and receive God's love and His gift of forgiveness.

May God bless you with His power, His love, His guidance, His resources, and His peace. No weapon formed against you or your loved ones will prosper (Isaiah 54:17a). May God's faithful promises be your armor and protection (Psalm 91:4c). May you and your loved ones escape any adverse situation safely and victoriously. May you walk into the fullness of God's love for you in Christ Jesus according to the Book of Ephesians Chapter 3 verses 16 - 21. May God's goodness and unfailing love pursue you all the days of your life (Psalm 23:6a). I pray all of these things in the matchless and mighty name of Jesus Christ!

Chapter 6

Overcoming Trauma

Trauma is a delicate topic to write about or to discuss. Many of us have faced trauma in some form or fashion. As human beings living in a dark and sinful world, most of us have experienced trauma. And for some, it even had a significant impact on us, so much that it reshaped how we think. Trauma can even affect how we interact with others. Trauma can be multidimensional and multigenerational. It can also be dangerous if we don't deal with it and its effects head-on.

In the late 17th century, the word *trauma* was generally used as a medical term in Latin. The usage of the word was to describe as a 'physical wound.' Nowadays, we use the word to refer not only to a physical state but also to an emotional and mental state. According to Dictionary.com, trauma is defined as a 'deeply distressing or disturbing experience.' These distressing and disturbing experiences can vary to many different things in our lives.

Sometimes life can throw one traumatic event at us after another. Throughout my life, I can see the traumatic events took a toll on me. Everything from witnessing abuse at an early age to grieving my brother's death during my young adult years became a traumatic wound in my heart. In those challenging moments, food became my self-medication and my comfort zone. I was so angry at God, I ignored Him and denied His love for me. I became hopeless.

I approached life with my sinful desires, fallible theology and tried to make my own rules. Deep inside, my soul was screaming and crying for a savior when I had a savior all along. His name is Jesus Christ.

Now you may be thinking, *if Jesus is a Savior, why didn't He save me from that heartbreak, that betrayal, or even when I was violated?* To be honest, I don't have a direct answer to the questions you may have. Some days I found myself asking God the same type of questions. One thing I do know is that we live in a broken and evil world. Ever since Adam and Eve sinned and disobeyed God's commandment of not eating from that specific tree, sin, brokenness, evil, and rebellion spread throughout the world (Genesis 1- 3, Romans 5:12). God knew that sin and rebellion would spread throughout the world, and that is why He sent His only Son, Jesus Christ, to die for our sins and to overcome death itself. Jesus is our beautiful gift from God and a representation of God's love and mercy towards us (Romans 5:15). And through Jesus Christ, and only through Him, we are saved (John 3:16, Romans 10:9).

There is hope in Jesus. He is our Triumph over trauma! The word triumph is used as a noun and a verb in the English language. As a noun, the word triumph is described as 'victory.' Jesus is our Victory over trauma! The definition of the word triumph as a verb means to prevail! Jesus is the One who helps us overcome trauma! And although Jesus can remove our storms, but may choose not to because He is sovereign, Jesus can give you wisdom and peace during our storms (Matthew 8:23 - 24, James 1:5-6, Philippians 4:6-7). Jesus may even invite us to walk on water in the midst of our storms (see Matthew 14:22 – 33).

Whether you are dealing with emotional storms, financial storms, relational storms, etc. Know that Jesus is the ultimate Waymaker! He has made and still is making a way out of no way.

He is the Breaker (Micah 2:13); He can break through every barrier and glass ceiling in your life! He is the One who prevailed for us! If you need comfort, call on Jesus. If you need counsel, call on Jesus. If you need a Savior, call on Jesus. He may not show up how we want Him to show up, but remember, His ways are higher than our ways, and His thoughts are higher than our thoughts (Isaiah 55:8-9).

We can find hope and stability in Jesus Christ. For He is God! We may be going around in circles, but GOD! God can lead us to His heart through Jesus Christ and His comfort through His Holy Spirit!

THE HOPE AFTER

Looking back at my life, I see how God has sent me so many different people and His Church to display His lovingkindness and mercy towards me. Over the past few years, Jesus led me to amazing counselors and therapists, supportive friends, phenomenal organizations, e-courses and books to help me process a lot of things in my life. He led me to so many great resources while showing me that He, Jesus Christ, is the Source! Jesus is truly the way, the truth, and the life (John 14:6a). If you need help and guidance, ask Him! He creates beauty from the ashes of our lives while also expanding His Kingdom on Earth. What a mighty and loving God we serve!

> Bless the LORD, O my soul, And forget not all His benefits: Who forgives all your iniquities, Who heals all your diseases, Who redeems your life from destruction, Who crowns you with lovingkindness and tender mercies, Who satisfies your mouth with good *things, So that* your youth is renewed like the eagle's.
>
> PSALM 103:2 - 5 NKJV

Being on the other side of trauma is powerful, especially when you're there with Jesus! You survived everything you went through! You survived the heartbreaks, the traumas, and even a pandemic! You made it here at this exact moment, at this exact time! See, that wasn't by accident! That wasn't just a coincidence. God has created you for such a time as time! So that, hopefully, you will be a part of His kingdom and His divine family by repenting and accepting Jesus Christ into your hearts. And to be a representative of His light here on Earth. And if you already accepted Jesus Christ as your Lord and Savior, this is an invitation to go deeper in your journey with Him, to be renewed by the Spirit of God from the inside out. There is a beautiful purpose for you to walk into for your good and for His glory. God has no favorites (Romans 2:11). If He can deliver and heal me from my past traumas to walk triumphantly in Him, He can do the same for you!

God created us to reflect a part of Him. In His Holy Word, He calls us MORE than conquerors (Romans 8:37)! He has a loving and powerful plan for you to live out (see Jeremiah 29:11). Usually, we don't walk into God's wonderous plan for us without first accepting Jesus into our hearts and lives by faith. We need His light to overcome the darkness! God's light is love, faith, hope, glory, and more. But where is God's light? It's in Jesus Christ!

Don't you see?! We are carrying parts of God inside of us because we were created in His image through Jesus Christ (see Genesis 1:27, John 1:3)! But we are truly light-barriers when we come to fully accept Jesus Christ as our Lord and Savior. Whether you see yourself as me, Sarah, Janah, Valerie, or Gregory in my story, if you're reading this now, God has a glorious and redemptive plan for you! Yes, YOU! God loves you so much that He sent His one and only Son to die for you. Jesus died on the cross for our sins and wrongdoings, was buried, and rose on the third day to overcome death for you. He loves you that much! That type of sacrificial love is rare, unique, and beautiful and is found in Jesus Christ. If you want to experience a love like never before in Jesus Christ, and you haven't put your heart and confidence in Him, just repeat out loud after me:

> *Jesus, I am so sorry and I repent for all of my sins and wrong-doings. I may not know You but by faith, I want to get to know you starting today. I want to get to know you as Savior, Brother, Leader, and Lord of my life. I believe by faith that You died, You was buried, and You rose again on the third day. I accept you as Lord over my life, right now, at this very moment. Thank You, Lord Jesus, for everything you've done for me and will continue to do in my life! In Jesus name, I say, Amen!*

And just like that you have been saved by God's grace! Welcome to being a light-barrier on earth! Welcome to God's kingdom and the Body of Christ! Congratulations!!! I am so excited for you!

I am praying for you and your new life as a child of God and a Believer of Jesus Christ! I pray over the next couple of months that you will experience amazing encounters with the Lover of your Soul, Jesus Christ! And He will lead you to a bible or a bible app, biblical community, God-fearing leaders/pastors after His own heart, and so much more! Spend the next couple of minutes, days, weeks, or months building your relationship with Him! By grace, He will lead you along the way of this beautiful journey!

And maybe you are already saved, this is an invitation to experience a beautiful *selah* moment, a divine pause. To dive deeper into your relationship with God! Let's go deeper into His Word and journey with the Spirit of God, and rely on Him more and more each day. Feel free to put the book down for a couple of hours or days to make room for God. This is a monumental point of your life, and I want you to experience every part of it! No person, book, job, show, social media, or anything else is more important than our relationship with Jesus! I'm super excited for you! See you soon Sis!

Chapter 7

Obedience over Everything

Welcome back! I hope you had a wonderful time with the Lord. I want to share with you why I entitled this section of the book, *Submit*. I called this section *Submit* because, over the past few years, God taught me how important it is to submit unto Him and the path He has for us. I saw myself trying to rebel my way out of the process of being developed by God. I loved my comfort zones more than I love choosing to follow God wholeheartedly. But thanks be to God for doing a miraculous heart transformation within me, where I now desire to obey God over everything else.

God requires us to live a life of obedience unto Him, just like Jesus did when He physically lived His life on Earth almost 2,000 years ago. Jesus' earthly life (described within the Books of Matthew, Mark, Luke, and John) gave us the blueprint for living a life of obedience. By studying the life and words of Jesus throughout the Bible, we can be better equipped to live a life of Christ-centered obedience. Sometimes it may be hard or intimidating to obey God fully and freely, but it is worth it! God can show us how to obey Him! We don't have to rely on our own strength. God gives us the gift of His Holy Spirit to lead us to live a life that honors Him. There is nothing like obeying and listening to God! Like the Word says, "Listen! Obedience is better than sacrifice" (1 Samuel 15:11b NLT). Obeying God is way better than any sacrifice we can offer Him or to others. It doesn't matter how great our sacrifices are if we are not submitted to God's voice and His instructions!

God began to lovingly show me how I can be strong-willed, defiant, and ignore His instructions. He instructed me to do something, and I do something else instead. Then God began to show me that any type of sacrifice doesn't replace the obedience God requires of us. Like toddlers, we can be stubborn, neglect His instructions, and be disobedient. We can sometimes give God adoration instead of obedience, praise instead of obedience, good works instead of obedience, and so on. That cycle in us needs to end now, in Jesus name! May we be attentive to God's instructions, quickly repent when we neglect them, and keep moving forward by the grace of God's Holy Spirit to obey Him. May we be more committed to obeying God over everything else, in Jesus mighty name!

> My dear children, I am writing this to you so that you will not sin. But if anyone does sin, we have an advocate who pleads our case before the Father. He is Jesus Christ, the one who is truly righteous.
>
> —1 JOHN 2:1

God is a just God! He is also merciful (Psalm 103:8). He won't leave you hanging. If He calls you to something, He will equip you through it! Remember, God loves us so much that He gave us His only Son, Jesus, to be our intercessor and our advocate.

Jesus wants our trust and confidence in Him. He also wants our attention. And I know it's hard, especially in this day and age, to give Him our full attention. But when we submit ourselves unto Him, He will empower us to seek Him wholeheartedly. In Matthew 6:33, it says, "But seek first the kingdom of God and His righteousness, and all these things will be provided for you." We don't have to walk in throughout this journey of life alone, Jesus wants to carry us along the way.

What has your attention nowadays, Love? Is it entertainment, social media, your job, your business, your family, your friends, etc.? What is it? How can you spend time with Jesus today, tomorrow, the next week, and the next month? It's not easy. Trust me, I know! But we have to make an effort every day. He wants our attention every day! Jesus wants a new and afresh YES unto Him every day. He has given us a new set of mercies and chances every morning (Lamentations 3:23); let's not take it for granted…

> Help us to remember that our days are numbered, and help us to interpret our lives correctly. Set your wisdom deeply in our hearts so that we may accept your correction.
> —Psalm 90:12 TPT

Following God's plans and His process will help us to become bold. If we don't submit to the steps God has for us to become bold, we risk missing the opportunity to be obedient unto God. We also may miss the opportunity to live a better life for ourselves, our children, and the future generation to come. Also, if we don't submit to the steps to becoming better, we may miss becoming the person God called us to be. We can also miss being there for the people who were connected to our lives.

Submitting to God's plan for our lives can be very practical as well as spiritual. If I didn't submit to the plan of going to Janah's house that night in December, I don't know where I would've been alive right now. If I did not submit to the leading of God to attend Epiphany Fellowship church that Christmas Sunday, then I probably would've been too emotionally tired to be resilient. My son, family, and other people would've felt the consequences of my lack of submission. Our daily decisions do not only affect us. They affect our family, our friends, and everyone connected to our lives. God will send His message through people, sermons, songs, or even social media posts to encourage us to submit unto Him. When we know what our divine, God-given instructions are, we owe it to ourselves and everyone connected to us to submit!

Jesus Christ experienced a life of submission on earth. When He was hours away from experiencing the most painful and shameful death and spiritual separation from God, He was deeply distressed to the point where He was sweating blood (Luke 22:44)! Yet, Jesus remembered His purpose, prayed, and submitted to His purpose (Hebrews 12:2, Luke 22:41 - 46)!

Maybe you don't know what your next heavenly instructions are. An excellent place to start is through prayer. God invites us to be ourselves while speaking to Him through prayer. There are many different ways we can communicate or pray unto God. And let us make room for Him to talk back unto us. God speaks to us in various ways, whether through His Word, people, dreams, visions, and more! One of the primary ways He can speak to us is through His Holy Word. The Bible is Jesus Himself (John 1:1). In The Book of John, Jesus said, "My sheep listen to my voice; I know them, and they follow me" (John 10:27 NLT). This is why it is vital to read or listen to the Bible.

Also, ask God for wisdom. God invites us to ask Him for wisdom, and He will give it to us generously if we do not doubt Him (James 1:5 - 6). Ask Him those tough questions. Like a wise woman once told me, He can handle your questions.

Without submission unto God, we risk not being our best selves for the One who created us. Like the Apostle Paul said, "But we are not like those who turn away from God to their own destruction. We are the faithful ones, whose souls will be saved" (Hebrews 10:39). Beautiful, God is calling you to come up higher with Him. He has called you to arise and to sit together in heavenly places with Jesus Christ (Ephesians 2:6)! Remember, we are called to be more than conquerors through Jesus, who loves us (Romans 8:37)! Let's dig deeper within ourselves, with the grace and leading of the Holy Spirit, to ask what do I need to do right now. This is a small, short, and powerful prayer: *Lord Jesus, I pray You will empower me to submit myself unto You. Not my will but let Your will be done. Realign my plans with Your purpose for my life, in Jesus name.* Asking God for the willingness to obey Him is bold and courageous in itself!

Also, another great strategy we can implement in the area of submission includes asking God about what our needs are in this season of our life. In Ecclesiastes Chapter 3, the author talks about how there is a time and season for everything. Identifying our need, time, and season through the lens of Jesus Christ can help us out in so many ways we can't even imagine. It is very critical to become aware of the times and seasons God has placed us in. Being aware of the times and seasons God has placed us in and our God-given specific assignments can help determine our next set of moves. God may call for a different thing in each season. God may be calling us into:

- a season of rest and being refresh in His presence
- a season of work and plowing in our work field
- a season of getting to know God for who He is
- a season of understanding and solidifying our identity in Jesus
- a season to study His Word
- a season of in-depth stewardship
- a season of deliverance and inner healing
- a season of meditating on God's Word
- a season of creating and innovation
- a season of transition

Or anything else God places on our hearts. This information may come through placing ourselves in devoted times of praise, prayer, fasting, reading the Word, and more. God's Holy Spirit may also talk to us as we walk in a Wal-mart parking lot or wash our dishes. You never know where or how you can hear the voice of God. The move of God cannot be traced or tracked down. At all times, we must be submissive to the move of the Holy Spirit, just like Jesus was during His time on earth! We must also submit to how God wants us to respond to the things He reveals to us. By embracing and submitting to God's purpose over our lives, we will be able to love and serve others well, just like Jesus! By doing this, we can live a bolder and better life!

Maybe Jesus is waiting for you to spend time with Him so that you can delight yourself in Him, and He can whisper the plans He has for you, in your heart, plans to prosper you and to give you a future full of goodness and hope (Jeremiah 29:11). Let us enter into the beauty and benefits of submitting unto God and His plans for our lives.

Chapter 8

Stand out in Character

As I mentioned earlier, our identity plays a pivotal role in understanding who we are and our purpose. Another key to becoming bold and unapologetically who we are is our character. According to the Merriam-Webster Dictionary, one of the definitions of character is *the complex of mental and ethical traits marking and often individualizing a person, group, or nation.* Our character is the very fabric of who we are, and it is an essential part of becoming bold. We must continually analyze, develop, and evolve in this aspect of our lives with the grace of God. It is crucial that we do not let our callings in life overshadow our character. Our character is the foundation of becoming bold. Author of *Urban Apologetics* and Pastor Dr. Eric Mason points out this crucial concept in his sermon series called Order In The Church (based on the Books of Timothy and Titus). He emphasizes how God always places one's character over competency! This means that God doesn't overlook our character even though each one of us is amazingly gifted and talented. God observes our character and hopes our character will reflect His.

We can see Jesus' Godly character beautifully and overtly highlighted throughout the Books of Matthew, Mark, Luke, and John.

Whether Jesus was interacting with women, children, those who were sick, or those in different ethnic groups, He emulated God's Spirit with kindness, gentleness, love, and so much more (Galatians 5:22-23). Jesus is and was clothed with strength, compassion, and humility, even choosing to honor those who dishonor Him (Luke 23:34). Although He was fully God and fully human on earth, Jesus didn't go around using His anointing and godliness for selfish reasons. Instead, He humbly submitted Himself to God the Father's purpose for Him while serving others (Philippians 2:5 - 8). Jesus is the epitome of what it means to have Godly character.

> Let this mind be in you which was also in Christ Jesus
> —Philippians 2:5 NKJV

Being bold is easier said than done. In a world where everything from social media to 'selfies', offers a false sense of confidence and validity, being bold in having Godly character can be very difficult. I know for me, it was easier to try to be like someone else than to be boldly and authentically myself. Standing tall in my shoes, in who God created me to be, was one of the most challenging things that I learned to do. But I thank God for His grace, guidance, and His patience in leading me on that journey of authenticity.

Learning my identity in Jesus Christ and being authentically myself has created a foundation for me. Through this foundation, my character began to form. Some of us have already mastered this area in our lives. We are bold; we aren't timid in expressing ourselves; we don't shy away from preaching the true Gospel of Jesus Christ. And some of us are still learning. Don't be so hard on yourself if you're still learning; repent and give yourself grace just like our Father in Heaven has already given you (Psalm 103: 8 – 13 NLT). We can ask God to deliver and heal us in those areas. Also, remember we cannot be slow in obeying God but instead let us continue preserving in growing in having Godly character.

When I began to find my identity in Jesus Christ, I realized how hard it was to express myself, especially in the area of faith. Being a dedicated follower of Christ isn't easy, nor is it simple, but it's worth it! The world rejected Christ, so in many ways the world will also reject us! As believers in Jesus Christ, we need to know that being rejected by this world will be normal. At school, at work, at home, in our families, we may be rejected. But I want to encourage you to stay strong and know that Jesus sees you and He loves you! Let's remember when our Lord and Savior Jesus said, "God blesses you when people mock you and persecute you and lie about you and say all sorts of evil things against you because you are My followers" (Matthew 5:11 NLT).

As we get rejected by different people within our lives, don't get discouraged! Forgive the person, if needed - confront the issue with pure and peaceful motives, let it go, pray for them, set boundaries as the Lord leads, and keep chasing after Jesus and His purpose for you! Do whatever the Spirit of God is leading you to do, and I would also encourage to maybe seek wise Godly counsel. Don't dim your light down for anyone! In the Word, it says that no slave is greater than his master (Matthew 10:24). So, if Jesus Christ was rejected, we will also be rejected when our identity is rooted in Christ. And yes, it's going to hurt being rejected not only by strangers but by some of the closest people we know, but it is worth shining the light Jesus placed inside of us. It is all worth it for God's glory!

See, our journey with Jesus isn't going to feel like a garden of roses all the time. The Christian walk is like a roller coaster. On a roller coaster, it feels exciting at first when we begin going uphill. Our hands may be in the air as we are feeling the excitement of being on the ride. Your hands might be on your head, so your wig won't fly off, or maybe that's just me. As the roller coaster continues, we reach a peak, and we may experience a calm moment while we feel the cool air on our faces. Then suddenly the roller coaster starts to go down the hill! We begin to feel the pressure of the speed of the coaster increasing as well as its kinetic energy. Instantly, we may feel dizzy and nauseous. We may even scream. At that moment, we can regret getting on the roller coaster. It might get so intense that we may even pass out. The ride isn't as exciting as it first was. It may become nerve-wracking. Our arms that were once in the air may be clinging on to the actual coaster for dear life.

Our Christian journey is filled with ups and downs, just like a roller coaster. It may feel exciting at some times and overwhelming at other times. But the one thing that remains consistent is that throughout the entire ride, The Manufacturer Himself, Jesus Christ, is with us during every moment of it all! He will never leave us, and He will never forsake us (Hebrews 13:5)

Our identity in Christ holds a piece of the puzzle to displaying God's glory on earth! Never shun your Godly character for anyone, anything, any corporation, culture, or institution. Turn to God with your heart, your hurts, your worries, requests, and concerns. Ask God to do a spring cleaning on your heart. Let us repent for our sins, break through every hindrance that may be holding us back from clinging unto God in the mighty name of Jesus! Place your cares on Him because He cares for you (1 Peter 5:7). Let us allow the Holy Spirit to speak to us, comfort us, and transform us into having the character of Jesus Christ. May we have the character for our God-given calling, in Jesus name! Be honest, stand up for what is right, show love and mercy to others. My friend, that's one of the boldest things we can do. This is how we stand out in character! Welcome to becoming BOLD!

Chapter 9

Moving in Faith

Faith is one of the main ingredients of submitting unto Jesus Christ. The word faith is mentioned over 300 times in the Bible (especially within the New King James Version of the Bible). It is mentioned most within the books of Romans and Hebrews. The Bible described faith as "the substance of things hoped for, the evidence of things not seen" (Hebrews 11:1 NKJV). Another version of this verse says, "faith comprehends as fact what cannot be experienced by the physical senses" (Hebrews 11:1c AMP). Author and Pastor Dr. Tony Evans describes faith as "acting like God is telling the truth." To me, faith is fully putting our hope, confidence, and trust in God. Whether we are moving forward in obeying God, maintaining Godly integrity in compromising situations, taking our thoughts captive (2 Corinthians 10:5), believing God for the things He promised us, or more, we need faith…

> And it is impossible to please God without faith. Anyone who wants to come to him must believe that He exists and that He rewards those who sincerely seek Him.
>
> —Hebrews 11:6 NLT

Moving in Faith

In the book of Hebrews Chapter 11, we see a list of people and the bold moves they made within their life! As we continue to read this chapter, we see the baseline of their bold moves was their faith in God. Their acts of faith were inspired by their belief in the character of God, what He instructed of them, the insight God revealed to them, or more. This chapter is commonly known as The Hall of Faith. Consider re-reading or listening through The Hall of Faith in The Book of Hebrews Chapter 11. Ask Jesus to show you something new while reading or listening to this chapter. Consider journaling what you learned. See how Jesus wants to enlighten and equip you in this passage. Starting today, we can choose to live a life of faith and obedience unto God! Our lives can be a beautiful hall of faith unto Jesus Christ for His glory alone!

After those tough seasons in my life, I felt the Lord calling me to follow Him. I obeyed and rededicated myself to Jesus Christ. I became serious about my walk with Him. I had to leave my old thought and toxic patterns behind and move into the new mindset and identity God had for me by faith. Jesus called me into a deeper journey with Him. And with His help, I answered the call, and I found myself doing many things by faith.

By faith, I invested in a study bible and began studying the Bible even when I didn't feel smart enough. By faith, I began going to therapy in the hope of becoming a healthy person. By faith, I began to enjoy my motherhood journey as a single mother. By faith, I began serving and leading others with joy as God instructed me to do even when I felt unqualified. By faith, I believed God's Holy Word and spoke His faithful promises over my son and I. By faith, I left relationships that did not please God and entered new relationships that honor God. By faith, I began writing my first self-published book to talk about the faithfulness of God as God instructed me, even when I didn't even have the official title for it. I also became a bolder and better woman, a writer and entrepreneur after I failed graduate school, and officially started a business during a pandemic by faith. By faith, I praised God and began to pray bold prayers as

He led me to do in times when I felt weighed down by anxiety and fear. By faith, the fervent prayers of the righteous have kept my family and I during difficult seasons (James 5:15). By faith, I overcame things I never thought I would've overcome. This was all done by God's love, mercy, and grace. He gave me the ability to trust Him over my understanding (Proverbs 3:5-6). I couldn't have done any of these things without God!

I thank God for equipping me with faith. I pray He will equip all of us with faith every day, in Jesus name! We need faith for the big things and the little things in our lives. Having faith in Jesus is to put our full trust, hope, and confidence in Him and His Word! Having faith in Jesus is to choose Him every day. Having faith in Jesus is giving Him our YES every day. Having faith in Jesus is to choose to submit to His will and way for our lives.

I can tell you right now, I am far from perfect. I need Jesus every day! I make mistakes, and sometimes I derailed from God's perfect plan for me. But that's when God's Holy Spirit convicts me and sometimes would send someone to preach, pray, or prophesy His word to me, guiding me to repent and to turn away from the sins I did. Then I would repent and actively realign myself back to Him. The Bible says that when we confess our sins, God is faithful to forgive us and clean us from all wickedness (1 John 1:9). Now I thank God for His mercy and forgiveness and continue to move in faith.

> O Sovereign LORD! You made the heavens and earth by your strong hand and great power and by your outstretched arm! Nothing is too hard for you!
>
> —Jeremiah 32:17 NLT

The truth is there is nothing too hard for God! If He can carry me through everything I went through, He can do the same for you! God has no favorites (Romans 2:11). If He did it for one, He could do it for another! There is no limitation or barriers in our lives that Jesus cannot breakthrough. There is nothing too hard for Him (Jeremiah 32:17).

THE EQUIPPING OF FAITH

Once we say with our mouths that Jesus is Lord and believe in our hearts that God raised Him from the dead (Romans 10:9), things change instantaneously in the spiritual realm! We become God's child by believing in His only Son, Jesus Christ. Other things, naturally, can take time to change. God's deliverance process can be instant, and His healing process can be over a period of time. That's why the Bible encourages us to do practical things such as:

- renewing our minds (Romans 12:2)
- meditating on Bible verses day and night (Joshua 1:8)
- putting all of our cares on God (1 Peter 5:7)
- thinking of what's holy, honorable, lovely, and pure (Philippians 4:8).

The Lord began to show me that repentance isn't just verbally say 'sorry' to Him, but true repentance is turning away from the sins that displease Him and walking out of God's standards by faith and the divine assistance of God's Holy Spirit!
    Within every stage of life, God can equip us with new levels of faith to obey Him and to believe in who He says He is! It takes faith to carry us from one place to another. God can give us that faith to take us from where we are now to where He wants us to be. Jesus said if we have faith as small as a mustard seed, we miraculously can uproot a mulberry tree (Luke 17:6). Meaning when we have faith, we can do amazing things and move in an atmosphere of signs, miracles, and wonder to glorify Jesus Christ on earth as He is glorified in Heaven (see John 14:12, 1 Peter 4:11). We can do all these things by faith, by putting our full hope and confidence in Jesus! Consider studying the life of Jesus in the Books of Matthew, Mark, Luke, and/

or John within the Bible; Jesus can also give us that faith to get to know Him in new ways we've never known Him before.

Our faith in God influences our belief systems and values. Then our belief systems and values can influence our thoughts and actions. This is why our faith in God is so important. God wants us to live out a life that honors and reflects Jesus Christ.

Believing that God is good and He wants good things for us can sometimes be tough, especially when so many things (including our personal life experiences) try to convince us that He is not good or maybe He doesn't care. But I'm here to tell you that God loves and cares about you so much that He sent His one and only Son to die for you. I heard a preacher once said if we were the only ones on earth, Jesus still would've died on the cross for us. Jesus would leave the 99 to go after you (Matthew 18:10 – 14). He loves us that much! It takes faith to believe in the Gospel of Jesus Christ, to believe that Jesus is good and Jesus is God, and that He has good plans for our lives. Yes, life will happen, the good and bad will occur in our lives, but Jesus' love for you and I will never change! Nothing can separate us from the love of Jesus Christ (Romans 8:35-39).

> Don't be faithless any longer. Believe!
> —JESUS CHRIST (JOHN 20:27C NLT)

Some common enemies that try to hold us back from moving in faith include doubt, fear, and unbelief. We all can experience them at some point in our lives, but if we embrace them, it can lead to sin and disobedience and can also put our future in danger. We can see detrimental consequences of doubt, fear, and unbelief throughout scripture (James 1:6, Matthew 13:58, Jude 1:5). I struggled with doubt, fear, and unbelief for many years. And Jesus showed me this ain't nothing to play with. Jesus is not complacent or passive when it comes to sin or the devil. In fact, Jesus came on earth to destroy the works of the devil (1 John 3:8). The devil is a defeated enemy. I had to stop being passive and complacent with sin in my life and reclaim the victorious authority that Jesus Christ gave me by being His follower (see Luke 10:19 and 1 Corinthians 15:57). Whatever is trying to hinder you from moving in faith as Christ is leading you, I pray God will reveal it to you and give the wisdom (James 1:5), strategy, the discipline, and the endurance to overcome it, in Jesus name.

One strategic way of overcoming the enemies of my faith is to fix my focus on Jesus is through the power of praise! Praise is magnifying Jesus Christ for who He is! We can praise Jesus through singing and dancing, writing, painting, and so much more! Who has Jesus shown you to be? To me, Jesus has shown me to be kind, loving, gentle, my savior, my master, my defender, my teacher, and so much more. Praise can be an essential tool for moving in faith and becoming a bolder and better woman! Praise can also be used as a spiritual weapon in a believer's life (we will discuss more spiritual weapons and spiritual warfare in Chapter 14 – Living in His Light). Look through your rapport with the Lord Jesus Christ and praise Him for who He is!

- In the pressure, praise Him!
- In the prison, praise Him!
- In the persecution, praise Him!
- In your purpose, praise Him!

Continue to walk by faith, Beautiful, and not by sight (2 Corinthians 5:7). Continue to praise by faith and not by sight. Remember that we are victorious in Christ Jesus! You are victorious in Christ Jesus (1 Corinthians 15:57)! Don't let your flesh, this world, or the devil hold you down! Thrive as a follower and friend of Jesus Christ!

> You see, every child of God overcomes the world, for our faith is the victorious power that triumphs over the world.
> —1 JOHN 5:4 TPT

Sometimes, we can mistakingly relate faith with a feeling. I used to wait to feel inspired before I moved in faith. But the Bible shows that faith is not a feeling but faith is an action. The action shows what or who we have faith in! Don't wait to feel faith, seek God and ask Him for an impartation! Let us not restrict faith with inspiration but let us connect faith to the implication of what God says to us! Like the Word of God says, "faith without works is dead" (James 2:17) but, in Jesus mighty name, may we have living faith and the works to match as we submit ourselves under the lordship of Jesus Christ.

Whether Jesus is directing us to exude love and peace while being single, to prepare for marriage when there is no mate in sight, leaving toxic habits and relationships, to work in diligence and excellence when we don't feel like it, to make a career switch or to ask for that promotion, to speak God's Word over your marriage and children when is chaotic, to start that business even though you didn't go to school for entrepreneurship, moving to a new place, or to invest in resources for the places He is sending us, whatever Jesus is instructing us to do, let us move boldly and joyfully in faith and submission unto Jesus Christ. And let us remain grateful while giving Jesus the glory, honor, and praise for it all!

And I know times are hard; if you need help, reach out for help. Ask God for help, ask your others for prayer, maybe consider investing in helpful resources, a mentor/coach, or counsel. (At the end of this book, there is a list of helpful resources that can assist you). You do not have to go through life alone. Dejection is not your portion! Depression is not your portion! I pray you will live and not die to see the goodness of God according to Psalm 27:13 in Jesus mighty name! I pray you can do all things through Jesus Christ who strengthens you according to Philippians 4:13. I pray God will send holy angelic & natural assistance to help you move in faith just like He did for Jesus when He chose to move in faith and submitted Himself to the will of His Heavenly Father (Matthew 27:32, Luke 22:43). I pray for all of these things, in Jesus name!

> So do not fear, for I am with you;
> do not be dismayed, for I am your God.
> I will strengthen you and help you;
> I will uphold you with my righteous right hand.
> —Isaiah 41:10

It can be hard to live by faith, especially when so much can be happening in our lives and even in the world! Know that Jesus is with us every step of the way. No matter what comes your way, know this truth: Jesus will never leave you, and He will never abandon you (Hebrews 13:5).

Let's keep our hearts open to Jesus' love. Our lives are so much more meaningful with Jesus in them and when we move in faith! And let us not shrink down because of fear or rejection of others. Let us remind ourselves that we would prefer to be rejected here on earth because of Jesus than to be rejected in front of God in Heaven (Matthew 10:33). Our obedience unto the Lord Jesus Christ will be worth it!

At least we know that when we face all of those things, we are not alone. We have an Advocate, a Best Friend, a Leader, the Great Shepherd, Jesus Christ Himself, who loves us and looks out for us! And we are guided by God's Spirit to move by faith in life with Jesus Christ right by our side! Let us be empowered by Christ's love for us to move in faith!

Chapter 10

Answer The Call

Jesus is calling us right now. He wants us to live a life that reflects a desire to please and honor Him (2 Timothy 1:9). With every call, there is an opportunity to respond. Even with God's power, strength, and might, He graciously gives us free will. He does not force us to do anything we don't want to do. There is an opportunity to choose between obeying and disobeying Him. Will you submit to Jesus' process for your life? Will I submit to Jesus' process for my life? Will we answer His call? I encourage you today, I'm encouraging all of us, to choose life by submitting unto Jesus Christ!

For a long time, I allowed fear and procrastination to hold me back—fear of becoming a single mother, fear of other's opinions, fear of the future, fear of failure, etc. The fear led to procrastination. God began to show me that I was submitting to the spirit of fear instead of submitting to Jesus. God has NOT given us a spirit of fear; instead, God gives us power, love, and a sound mind (2 Timothy 1:7). God's Word says that perfect love expels all fear (1 John 4:18). For His Word also says, "be bold and courageous, do not be afraid or discouraged. For the Lord is with you wherever you go" (Joshua

1:9). Believing and receiving these truths in my heart and mind has equipped me to overcome fear and answer God's calling over my life!

My dear sister, do not let fear, pride or anything else hold you down or hold you back! Repent and renounce all sin patterns in your life. This is the time for you to arise and shine (Isaiah 60:1)! The world needs to hear and see you! In God's brilliant mind, He wanted and chose to create you for such a time as this! Abide in God's shelter through prayer (Psalm 91:1)! His faithful promises are your armor and protection (Psalm 91:4). Be bold, in Jesus name! Be courageous in doing the things God has told you to do. Be courageous in being the person God has called you to be, in Jesus name! Put on the full armor of God as mentioned in Ephesians Chapter 6 verses 13 – 17 and go where the Lord is sending you! Answer the calling of God over your life for Jesus Christ glory alone!

> is my command—be strong and courageous! Do not be afraid or discouraged. For the LORD your God is with you wherever you go."
> —JOSHUA 1:9 NLT

When we put our hope in Jesus Christ, we become a new creation in Him. The old things have passed away, and He begins to do a new work inside of us (2 Corinthians 5:17, Isaiah 43:18-19). Although this type of transition can be difficult, this transition is beautiful!

Every time I think about this, I think of salmon. A few months ago, I learned that usually salmon fishes are born in the river. And after birth, they swim downstream to live in the ocean, spending most of their lives there. When it is time to give birth or spawn, they swim upstream to the exact place they were born to give birth and then die immediately afterward. This is a beautiful illustration of how we should walk out our lives. When we give our lives to Jesus Christ, we must also trace our steps to the Designer of our souls, the Creator of the Universe, The Most High God, God Almighty, to gain insight into who He is and the purpose He gave us before we were placed in our mother's womb (Jeremiah 1:5). When we go back into His presence, a divine transformation happens. Our old self dies, and we become new in Jesus Christ. It is only through Jesus Christ that we have access to God Himself (John 14:6).

Once we began to acknowledge and understand who God formed us to be, it's our job to steward and manage what He placed inside of us. It is our job to share it with others as the Lord leads. For example, I recently learned that God placed a piece of His joy inside of me. He created me to help spread His joy on earth to ultimately point others back to Jesus. That's how God built me. What if I took all that joy and refused to share it with others? What will be the point of putting all of that joy inside of me? God wants me to share what He created inside of me with others.

What has God placed inside of you to share with the world? During your time of prayer, ask Jesus how He created you and what attributes He placed within you. What are some positive attributes others compliment about you? Maybe consider asking 2 – 4 people in your life to describe you in three positive words; what words did they pick to describe you? Ask God in prayer if those words align with how He created you and the attributes He placed inside of you. I received clarity, vision, and book ideas in the place of prayer! Even as you read the Bible, specific passages and stories may awake a passion in you. These passages and stories that you feel passionate about may point to the calling or gifts God has placed inside of you.

Years later, the Lord Jesus Christ began to show me the concept of dichotomy and how the enemy tries to use the opposite attribute of those beautiful traits God gave us to destroy us back. During those tough times in my life, the devil tried to overtake me with misery (the opposite of joy). But Jesus was and is with me every step of the way, just like He is with you every step of the way. He even rescued me and led me to great resources and counselors to walk through that misery. After a few months, I became filled with joy and began to love again. Now I am writing this book to empower you, through the power of Holy Spirit, to help you face whatever you may be facing! I don't know what the enemy is using to hold you back in life, but I pray that no weapons formed against you shall prosper in Jesus name (Isaiah 54:17a). May God give you more and more mercy, peace, and love according to Jude 1:2 in Jesus name! What the enemy meant for evil, Jesus wants to turn it around for good in your life and to help others through your breakthrough (Genesis 50:20)! Jesus is amazing! May He constructed a divine reversal in our lives! Hallelujahh! Thank you Jesus!!!

The Process

Being bold is truly a transitional process; it doesn't happen overnight. Learning how to submit to Jesus' plans for our life is not easy. But it is worth it! One key to submitting unto Jesus Christ is having the willingness to submit.

Submitting to God's will for my life wasn't easy but I was and am willing to submit my life unto God. Jesus showed us how to submit willingly unto while He physically lived on earth. We see a paramount picture of Jesus speaking unto God as His Heavenly Father, submitting His desires for God's desires for His life, and surrendering His desires to follow the leading of God's Holy Spirit! Before His excruciating death on the cross for the hope that we may answer God's call for us, Jesus prayed this powerful prayer of submission and surrendering unto God, saying "nevertheless not My will, but Yours, be done." (see Luke 22:42 NKJV). There, the Lord gave us words and insight on how to pray in the midst of the process of submission. Jesus even submitted to the process of overcoming death itself after resurrecting on the third day!

Observing Jesus' level of submission empowers us to live out a submissive life! Our journeys of submitting unto God will look different, and your path to becoming bold does not have to look like others. God is cultivating something new and unique inside each of us who placed our trust in Jesus, so we can ultimately look more like Jesus and bring His kingdom down on earth as it already is in Heaven (Matthew 6:10).

One way of submitting to God's plan on earth as it's already established in Heaven is through prayer. Prayer is having an honest and humble conversation with God. In prayer, God can reveal His purpose for our lives, our families, our communities, and this world! And I thank God it doesn't take big and fancy words for God to hear us. Our prayers can be short and simple, as long as it's honest. Some prayers I prayed during that dark season of my life, was "Jesus please give me wisdom" or "Jesus help me." And somedays I didn't even have the words to pray, I just cried. God saw my every tear (Psalm 56:8). By His mercy and grace, He heard my cry!

> The LORD is close to the brokenhearted; he rescues those whose spirits are crushed.
> —PSALM 34:18

God hears you, Love! He sees you! Cry out to Jesus and allow Holy Spirit to lead you in prayer! You can pray in your car or your kitchen while you're cooking. You don't have to kneel with your hands folded to pray. God is not looking at our physical posture, but He is watching the posture of our hearts. He wants to hear our beautiful voices speaking to Him!

As we submit unto Jesus Christ, distractions will begin to appear. Distractions can seem "beneficial" to us or "good" for us. The distractions can be our fleshly desires and can disguise themselves as divine opportunities from God. But it takes discernment to distinguish what is from Jesus Christ and what is from our flesh or the devil. The Bible mentions in 2 Corinthians 11:14, that even Satan disguises himself as an angel of light. But praise be to God that Jesus defeated Satan and stands victorious to this day (Colossians 2:13-15, Revelation 1:18)! My dear sister, when we are in Christ Jesus and chooses to follow Him, we are victorious over Satan and his temptations. Let us protect our hearts and focus. Let us walk in our authoritative victory given to us by Christ Jesus, in Jesus mighty name!

> But thanks *be* to God, who gives us the victory through our Lord Jesus Christ.
> —1 Corinthians 15:57

In conclusion, we saw the importance of speaking to God as our Heavenly Father and speaking His Word over us during the first section of the book. Then we discussed the significance of submitting ourselves unto Jesus during the second section of the book! Next, we will explore the concept of surrendering unto God's Holy Spirit. These are vital parts of experiencing and becoming a bolder and better version! There is a calling to submit, Beautiful. Will you answer the call?

Section III

Surrender

Chapter 11

Purpose and Prudence

Surrender was a tough concept for me to understand. When I researched the word, it can describe it as 'giving up rights,' or generally 'to lose.' In essence, according to Dictionary.com, surrender means 'to yield (something) to the possession or power of another.' You may be thinking, *what does surrender have to do with becoming bold*? A couple of years ago, I heard of the word 'surrender' within the context of leaving a toxic relationship, I was so confused. A relationship coach was telling a woman to surrender after a difficult break-up. '*What?*', *'Why does a person have to surrender after a relationship as if they were in a war?* I thought. But that's exactly what a toxic relationship is, a war!

There is a war happening. A war between our old self and our new self. A war between old habits and new ones. A war between an old mindset that may permit pain and chaos, and a new mindset that sets boundaries and boldly displays self-compassion in every area of life. And even beyond that, it is a war between the enemy's purpose and God's purpose over our lives. Whether it's within our relationships, our health, finances, emotions, or environments, God wants us to flourish in His goodness and lovingkindness through

Jesus Christ. God's perfect will is for our soul to prosper so we can glorify Jesus fully & freely on the earth while serving others excellently (see 3 John 1:2).

We won't be able to win any war if we are ill-equipped for the battles. (Later in Chapter 14, Living in His Light, we will discuss specific spiritual weapons to be equipped for spiritual warfare). Thank God, Jesus already won the war for us and gained the victory! To win the battles in our lives, we must begin and continue seeking Jesus first and surrender to His Spirit. To successfully surrender is to give up our rights, our will, our desires for God's desires, His will, and His way. He wants us to give up every part of my life to Him. Everything from certain emotions to sometimes even physical things. To stand before Him completely vulnerable and allowing Him to cover us (see Zechariah 3)! By surrendering to God's Holy Spirit, we allow God's Holy Spirit to guide our every direction and step.

> Beloved, I pray that you may prosper in all things and be in health, just as your soul prospers.
> —3 John 1:2 NKJV

In those moments of surrendering, God provides stability throughout this intense journey called life! Without any stability in our lives, we can easily become moved by the waves of life. We need to stand our ground and grabbed onto something. Well, more like SOMEONE! Someone who is unchangeable! Someone who is the same yesterday, today, and tomorrow (Hebrews 13:8). That someone is Jesus, Our Mighty Anchor! In Jesus, there is stability. In Jesus, there is purpose! In Jesus, there is perfect rest and comfort. In Jesus, there is perfect peace! For He is called the Prince of Peace (Isaiah 9:6). In Him, there is all of that and more!

With the knowledge and understanding of God as our Heavenly Father, Jesus Christ as our Lord and Savior, and God's Holy Spirit as our Helper and Guide, we can boldly begin walking in the purpose and callings God has for us! As believers of Jesus Christ, we all have a collective purpose to fulfill. This purpose is to make disciples of Jesus Christ and more (see Matthew 28:19 – 20). Whether in our homes, our families, our jobs, our businesses, our ministry, our schools, or within any environment the Lord has called us to, we can fulfill this purpose in our lives.

How we uniquely fulfill our purpose is our calling. God calls each one of us (2 Timothy 1:9). Whether we are sisters, friends, wives, mothers, students, leaders, mentors, employees, employers, and so on, God's Holy Spirit wants to partner with us and lead us to help fulfill His purpose on the earth. God welcomes us to ask about how we can uniquely fulfill this purpose in our lives. Not knowing our purpose, mission, and "why" can lead us to do reckless things. Not knowing and embracing our purpose and callings can even have us going back to those toxic cycles God delivered us from.

Many times, I was tempted to go back into the toxic relationship I had with Gregory, I was even tempted to start dating aimlessly while compromising my values and boundaries. Sometimes I would overcome those temptations, and one time I fell into that temptation. It was 10 months after those dark days in December, I had a chance to see Gregory again. And even though, I had boundaries in place, and I was living for God, one thing led to another, and I had sex with him. I fell for the temptation. Immediately, I was so heartbroken about that decision. I felt like I took ten steps forward in God and twenty steps back after that one decision, after that one sin. But God still led me to repent and chose to forgive me out of His grace and mercy. While reading a verse in the Book of Jeremiah, I felt God's Holy Spirit clearly warning me not to have sex outside of marriage again! After that, I restarted my boundaries with Gregory and told him we could never reenter a romantic relationship again due to the toxic behaviors and patterns we both had within the relationship.

Then, I began to study the concepts of boundaries, what they are and how to establish them. I also began listening through an audiobook book called Boundaries by Dr. Herny Cloud. I felt like God's Holy Spirit wanted me to read this particular book a few months before committing that sexual sin. While going through the book, I learned a lot about creating boundaries, maintaining boundaries, and the importance of boundaries from a Christ-centered perspective. I began to learn that surrendering to God's Holy Spirit is super vital during my walk with Jesus Christ. And from there, Holy Spirit began to develop His fruit within my character. Holy Spirit's fruit consists of love, joy, peace, kindness, goodness, faithfulness, gentleness, and self-control (Galatians 5:22-23). If one chooses not to walk in Holy Spirit's fruit (regardless of how gifted they are), they become a worker of iniquity, as Christ mentioned in Matthew chapter 7. Throughout Jesus' life on earth, we see Jesus walking out each part of this fruit. Jesus truly showed us what it means to live a purposeful and prudent life!

> "Now you are well; so stop sinning, or something even worse may happen to you."
> —JESUS CHRIST (JOHN 5:14)

Holy Spirit led me to read that verse one day in the Book of John Chapter 5, and it spoke to me. It helped me to truly repent. Years later, God is keeping me and generously gives me His strength. I truly thank God for a Jesus-loving, God-fearing, Holy Spirit-following biblical type of community who kept me accountable, prayed for my deliverance and inner healing, and helped me overcome those temptations. I thank God for my friends who lovingly challenged me and reminded me that I came too far to compromise my future. Since then, by God's grace, I haven't returned to that toxic cycle of having sex outside marriage, and I did not reenter the romantic relationship I had with Gregory. Years later, Gregory and Valerie gave their lives unto Jesus Christ and accepted Jesus as Lord and Savior!

No matter what you have done last month, last week, yesterday, or even today, God still wants to choose you to display His goodness and grace upon the earth. Turn away from that sin, Beautiful, whatever that sin may be. Whether it's fornication, pride, etc., turn away from it and truly repent from those sins. Receive God's holy forgiveness. Surrender to God's Holy Spirit today. Accept the gift of repentance and enter into a time of refreshing with God (see Acts 3). I need God all day, every day. By God's Holy Spirit, I am led to repent for my sins as much as I can because I truly cannot live a Godly life without Him. And even within my mess, He still chose to use me for His glorious purpose. As you are reading this, God still wants to use you as His instrument for His marvelous purposes on earth.

I pray God will get the glory out of your story and out of your willingness and obedience unto Him. Your obedience unto God is not in vain! I also pray He will send you and continue to nourish Christ-centered community in your life who are not afraid to tell you the truth in gentle love (see Galatians 6:1). Having a Christ-centered community is an extension of God's grace and love for us. Let us treasure our community given to us by God. Life is too hard to go through it alone.

Embracing Prudence

As we move forward in God, let's try to remember what's at stake with every decision we make. When we don't consider our future, we can risk hindering our destiny. In the past, I made the mistake of not considering how my decisions affect my future as well as my son's future. Now I try to consider my son's future, my future, and even other people's lives connected to mine before making a decision. Over the past few years, Holy Spirit has been teaching me the concept of prudence. According to the Merriam-Webster dictionary, prudence is defined as the ability to govern and discipline by the use of reason. Prudence is also defined as the sagacity in the management of affairs and caution as to danger or risk. There are so many bible verses about being prudent, especially throughout the Book of Proverbs (Proverbs 8:12, Proverbs 13:16, Proverbs 27:12). Jesus talked about the concept of being prudent throughout His earthly ministry, especially in Matthew Chapter 25.

One of His most famous parables, The Parable of the Ten Talents, is found in Matthew Chapter 25. Jesus described three different servants who were given a different amount of money, also known as talents, from their master. The first two servants used their time, energy, and talents wisely and multiplied the talents their master had given them. The third servant hid his talent in the ground. When the Master came back from his journey, he was pleased with the first two servants and rewarded them for being excellent managers of their time, energy, and resources. And to the third servant, he was greatly displeased with him for hiding his talent, calling him "wicked and lazy."

The first two servants showed us that our time, our energy, our resources are valuable. This parable also helps us reevaluate to see if we are giving our Lord and Savior Jesus Christ a great ROI (return of investment) with the time, energy, and resources He has given us. This entire chapter in Matthew 25 is so rich with so many lessons and gems. The chapter speaks on the concept of being prudent and how to live our lives for Jesus Christ with intentionality. I would encourage all of us re-read Matthew 25 for ourselves and ask God's Holy Spirit to open up our eyes to see what He wants us to see. And to open up our eyes to hear what He wants us to hear.

Embracing prudence is the concept of being wise and taking account of the future. Being prudent is thinking of the end goal in mind and having that become a factor in our decision-making today. It is thinking about what matters the most, honoring Jesus Christ above all throughout our lives. It is vital to be prudent in reaching our God-given purpose. Reflecting on how our decisions can affect our futures can help us becoming more of a prudent woman. We think beyond how our decisions can affect us today and see how our seemingly small decisions today can affect us 2, 5, and even in eternity. Some of us have already mastered this concept of prudence, and some of us are still learning. It's all grace! Continue to go and flow where God's Holy Spirit is leading you. Continue to flourish in God's lovingkindness and goodness, Beautiful! We going to make mistakes, but hopefully we can quickly learn from our mistakes and the mistakes of others. And let's ask for help when we need it to get the wisdom we need to make wiser decisions.

God speaks life into us and validates us by telling us how and why He created us. God created each and every one of us for a specific reason. We are not created by accident or mistake. God loves us and has a purpose for us before the foundations of time (Jeremiah 1:5).

Before we can be bold in our God-given purpose, first we need to receive clarity regarding our purpose. There is a famous Zig Ziglar quote that says "if you aim at nothing, you will hit it every time." It is important for us to be intentional regarding achieving our purpose. As believers of Jesus Christ, our purpose includes sharing the *true* Gospel of Jesus Christ which is found in Romans 10:9, and its purpose in John 3:16. I emphasize the word 'true' because there can be a false gospel. A false gospel can be centered on other things outside of Jesus Christ. The true Gospel of Jesus Christ is centered by the name and nature of Jesus Christ. The true Gospel of Jesus Christ portraits God's truth, perfect love, righteousness, peace, and joy (Romans 14:17). We should always be led by the administrative authority and grace of Holy Spirit in fulfilling our purpose. While we are achieving our purpose, we should remember this truth, we are not abandon but accompanied by our Lord and Savior Jesus Christ Himself (Matthew 28:20).

> Jesus came and told his disciples, "I have been given all authority in heaven and on earth. Therefore, go and make disciples of all the nations, baptizing them in the name of the Father and the Son and the Holy Spirit. Teach these new disciples to obey all the commands I have

given you. And be sure of this: I am with you always, even to the end of the age."
—JESUS CHRIST (MATTHEW 28:18 - 20 NLT)

Many resources are available to us when it comes to finding our callings. Some helpful resources that assist me in becoming more prudent and purposeful in my life included: doing SWOT analysis on different areas of my life, getting therapy, hiring a life coach, journaling, using a timer while working on a task, and more.

Other resources can also help give us the vocabulary and language to who we are and how God created us. These personality assessments benefited me in giving me clarity in the area of my personality make-up. These personality assessments include:

- DISC Personality Test
- Gallup's CliftonStrengths (StrengthsFinder) Test
- Myers Briggs Type Indicator
- Truity: Career Personality Profiler Test

At the end of this book, there is a list of resources that can assist you in your journey to finding your unique calling. Before utilizing these resources, I want to emphasize never to put any resources before the Source – God. I invite you to dive deeper into God's Holy Word, study Jesus' character, and ask God for a filling and a surrender to His Holy Spirit. Through prayer, within God's presence, is where He affirmed me and validated me with who I am in Him and with the vocabulary of my calling. Sometimes they are hindrances in the way of seeing what God wants to do inside of us and through us. I pray for God to deliver us from all forms of evil so we can fully flourish as the women of God we are called to be, in the mighty name of Jesus! If the Son sets you free, you are free indeed (John 8:36).

Looking at different interests and passions can be one of the ways Holy Spirit can point us to our God-given calling, but God is limitless, and He wrote a story for us regardless of our past interests and passions. There may be a temptation to envy or copy someone's else calling but let us overcome that temptation and seek clarity straight from the Source Himself – Holy Spirit. We need to ask Him what His holy will for our lives is. Even though His sovereignty may sometimes feel scary, He loves us with an everlasting love and wrote our stories with the pen of perfect love. Jesus is the Author and Finisher of our faith (Hebrews 12:2)! We can find comfort in that. The same calling He had placed inside of us before He placed us in our mother's womb is the same story He wants for us now, regardless of our past mistakes! But we can only see that calling manifest if we fully and freely surrender to God's Holy Spirit through accepting Jesus Christ in our lives as our Lord and Savior. Every other way to God and our purpose is a counterfeit and will ultimately lead to destruction.

Jesus has given us each a great purpose and commission as His followers. And each of us is chosen to uniquely express our God-given purpose. Our purpose can be expressed by being an excellent employee on our job who is integral and never denies the name of Jesus or that friend who displays God's love and grace through their actions to others. Whether we are being gracious and loving friends, honoring our spouse, raising our children, starting a ministry, being an excellent employee at our jobs, and/or becoming an entrepreneur, we can fearlessly fulfill our God-given purpose. Remember, we are wonderfully created in God's image, and we are multifaceted. You can do all things through Christ who strengthens you (Phil. 4:13). God calls us to carry out that Matthew 28 mandate in various ways through our callings. I thank God He gave us His Spirit, Holy Spirit, to lead us and empower us to do that. Let us continue to seek God's Holy Spirit and ask Him for direction in our lives, endurance to do what He has called us to do while surrendering it all unto Him. Holy Spirit will give us unique ideas and strategies to draw us closer to Him!

> But the Helper, the Holy Spirit, whom the Father will send in My name, He will teach you all things, and bring to your remembrance all things that I said to you.
> — Jesus Christ (John 14:26 NKJV)

That is one of the beauties of surrendering unto God's Holy Spirit. He is so innovative, brilliant, and unique! He is the Spirit of Truth, and reveals God's Truth to us! He helps us become more prudent regarding our purpose to live a bold and better life that glorifies our Lord Jesus Christ!

Chapter 12

The Keys

Major key elements can contribute to becoming more of a surrendered woman unto God's Holy Spirit. As a former control freak, these things really helped me in my journey of surrendering unto God. These key elements include resting, humility, the fear of the Lord, and much more. Throughout this chapter, we will be focusing on the first three: resting, humility, and the fear of the Lord.

Key #1 - Rest

Rest is essential to us flourishing as surrendered women of God. Everything from physically resting to emotionally resting is vital for our well-being. Staying still and resting can be difficult for some of us, especially when there is so much to do, but we should try our best to prioritize it. When we are not well-rested, we run the risk of not being the best version of ourselves at home, at work, and so on. This is why resting when it's time to rest is so important to do to become a bolder and better version of ourselves.

There are many different definitions of rest. The word can be used as a noun or an action verb. Although we usually associate the word 'rest' with the state of physically sleeping, the word has many different definitions and meanings. Let us dive deeper beyond the physical state of resting and talk about how our inner-beings also need rest. According to Merriam- Webster's dictionary, one of the definitions of rest is 'to be free from anxiety or disturbance.'

Can you remember the last time you rested? Not sleep, but actually rested? We can see the drastic changes in our physical being when we are deprived of sleep. Many research studies show that when we lack sleep, it takes a toll on our physical health and our emotional, mental, and even psychological health. If we know about these destructive effects from lack of sleep, how much more damage can a lack of rest do to our souls? This is why it is important to rest in God's presence. Whether we are resting and abiding in God's presence during our lunch break, while the kids at napping, during a staycation/ vacation, or more, we should continuously prioritize our time with God. Resting in God's presence can give us a chance to rejuvenate our minds, body, and our soul!

In the Old Testament, God instructed the Israelites to have one day of rest. This day is called the Sabbath (Exodus 20:8 – 11). The purpose of the Sabbath was also to acknowledge God for who He is, remove the cares of this world, and place Him back on the throne of His people's hearts. The Sabbath was a day that was also reflective of how God rested on the seventh day after He created the earth (Genesis 2:3). This Sabbatical format points us back to how vital resting and communing with God is and how much our souls need to spend time with Him.

Jesus painted this beautiful picture of resting. He protected and persevered His prayer time with Our Heavenly Father (see Luke 5:16). He even spent all night praying to the Father (Luke 6:12). Jesus showed us how to rest by prayer and communing with God in His presence. Jesus displayed what the Sabbath looked like, and He also fulfilled the Sabbath law by being the Master of the Sabbath. In the book of Matthew, Jesus states that He is the Lord of the Sabbath (Matthew 12:8)! Now we don't have to wait until the seventh day to rest or celebrate the Sabbath since we are in a new promise and covenant with Jesus Christ as Christians. Once we rest in Jesus Christ and worship Him, we will be entering into a sabbatical time with Him. When we honor and abide in Jesus Christ, by the leading of God's Holy Spirit, we will feel refreshed, renewed, and restored. In Jesus' presence, there is fullness of joy and treasures forevermore (Psalm 16:11).

Our boldness is connected to this concept of rest. This is so crucial to understand! If we overlook this essential part of our lives, we risk not transforming into the bold and better person God has called us to be! This will also potentially result in missing out on our God-given destiny! In the Old Testament, the children of Israel were promised by God of land with God's rest and His perfect plans for them. This land was called the Promised Land. But first, they were freed from their oppressors, the Egyptians, with God's power, might, signs and wonders. Also, they had to journey through unfamiliar lands, also known as the wilderness (Exodus 15). Through many tests and trials, complaining, embodying unbelief and disobedience, and ultimately rejecting God, the generation of rescued His people from Egypt did not make it to the Promised Land (except two people, Joshua and Caleb), but their children did (Numbers 14, Jude 1:5).

This shows us that when a person continues to be disobedient without turning away from their sinful ways, it will only lead to their own demise. But this will not be our portion, in Jesus name! May we continue to walk by faith and not draw back. May we not be like those who turn away from God to their own destruction but instead, may we become the faithful ones, whose souls will be saved according to Hebrews 10:38 - 39 in Jesus name!

While we aren't living under oppressors in Egypt, some of us live under our soul's oppressors: sin, pride, greed, laziness, the lusts of life, demonic oppression, and so much more. Like Moses, Jesus was sent on earth to deliver us from our oppression of sin and the devil. Jesus' earthly ministry led the movement of delivering us from these enemies of our soul. This was the goal of Jesus' ministry to do Father God's will by destroying the devil's works (1 John 3:8). By believing in the death, burial, and resurrection of Jesus and using the authority God gives us, we become victorious over the spiritual enemies of our souls that want to destroy us. It is through Jesus Christ, in whom we experience a divine transformation from victims to victorious!

> For the LORD your God is going with you! He will fight for you against your enemies, and He will give you victory!
> —DEUTERONOMY 20:4 NLT

Journeying to our own 'promised lands' that God has for us can be scary to some of us and exciting to others. The 'promise land' is not a literal place or location. To the children of Israel, it was. And to some of us, it can be. Whatever God has planned for you is for you! Being rightly aligned with the place, space, and timing of God's Holy Spirit is our promise land. Ultimately, being with Jesus Christ is our promise land. Although transitioning from one stage of life to another can be scary for some of us, there is comfort in knowing that God will never leave us nor forsake us (Hebrews 13:5c). Our prayer in this time of transition can be: Not my will, but let Your will, Holy Spirit be done in my life, in Jesus' mighty name!

God is so powerful and sovereign that He can restore us when we are resting in His presence. Whether it's in a specific season of our lives or in a season of transition, God wants to continue to do a beautiful work in us and through us. Sis, there is a purpose for our rest!

KEY #2 - HUMILITY

Being bold is amazing, but it is also nothing if we are not humble. Humility is another key concept of becoming bold! Some people look at a bold person as someone who disregards others' feelings, loud, bossy, controlling, and/or demeaning. That's not boldness, that's arrogance. We should be careful that we do not confuse the two. You can have a quiet and introverted-like personality and still be bold in God's eyes. Also, humility is not downplaying or spiritually gaslighting what God placed inside us. In addition to that, humility is also not exalting our shortcomings over what God says about us. That is false humility and pride.

True humility is for our character to reflect the character of Jesus Christ! True humility is also seeing others and ourselves how God sees us. True humility is submitting to our leaders (Romans 13:1-7, Hebrews 13:17) without denying the name of Jesus Christ and our Christ-centered values (see Daniel 3, Acts 5:17-42). True humility is having a mind like Jesus Christ, a mind that is focused on doing God's will and serving others (Phillippians 2) with compassion while giving Jesus all the glory, honor, and praise. Whether serving our spouses, our family, friends, communities, coworkers, and clients, serving God's Church, and/or our country, there is always an opportunity to serve. Humility is necessary for pleasing God with everything that we do (Ephesians 4:2, 1 Peter 5:5). It takes reliance on Holy Spirit to be authentically humble.

> In the same way, you who are younger must accept the authority of the elders. And all of you, dress yourselves in humility as you relate to one another, for "God opposes the proud but gives grace to the humble."
>
> —1 PETER 5:5 NLT

Humility is defined as "the quality of not being proud because you are aware of your bad qualities." A similar word to humility is meekness. Meekness, also known as gentleness, is a part of the Holy Spirit's fruit (see Galatians 5:22 – 23 KJV). When we are in God, abide in Jesus, and obey Holy Spirit, we produce good spiritual fruits (John 15). The nine parts of Holy Spirit's fruit are evident through our words, thoughts, and actions. The nine part of Holy Spirit's fruit includes love, joy, peace, patience, kindness, goodness, faithfulness, gentleness, and self-control (Galatians 5:22-23). Bearing the fruit of the Holy Spirit comes from spending time with God and obeying Him. That is the foundation of becoming bold and living a more fruitful life. This whole process is not only for our souls, but it is also to lay the foundation for our lives, character, gifts, breakthroughs, and so much more! In addition, being bold means being humble to let our Heavenly Father use us as His holy instruments, playing His beautiful melodies on the earth. Becoming bold is not only for ourselves but also for helping others in different areas of their lives, helping them to break free from limitations, and being all of whom God called them to be! Being authentic humble is a key to living out a bolder and better life!

Key #3 – Fear of the Lord

The fear of the Lord is holy fear and respect unto God. It's telling God that we don't want no problems with Him by our words, deeds, and actions. The fear of the Lord is a sobering and respectful mindset of acknowledging God's holiness. It is mentioned throughout the Bible. It is mentioned over 100 times in the Bible, and it is mentioned most in the Book of Proverbs. The fear of the Lord is having a holy fear and reverence for God. Having the Fear of the Lord is vital in becoming a bolder and better versions of ourselves because it affects how we interact with God and others. The Fear of the Lord brings sobriety to our thoughts, words, and actions. Holy Spirit helps us in this area by bringing up God's standard, Word, and holy conviction in our soul. He also equips us with the Fear of the Lord to remind us of what's most important, honoring and glorifying Jesus Christ.

> The [reverent] fear of the LORD [that is, worshiping Him and regarding Him as truly awesome] is the beginning *and* the preeminent part of wisdom [its starting point and its essence], And

> the knowledge of the Holy One is understanding *and* spiritual insight.
> —Proverbs 9:10 AMP

The Bible mentions multiple times that the fear of the Lord is the beginning of wisdom (Proverb 1:7, Proverb 9:10a, Psalm 111:10). So in order to gain Godly wisdom, we must have the fear of the Lord. But it is by Holy Spirit that we can have the fear of the Lord. The fear of the Lord is a part of Holy Spirit (see Isaiah 11:2), and we need to Him to have this key element in our lives. As we continue to surrender unto God, we will see the growth in this key element into becoming a bolder and better versions of ourselves. Continue to surrender unto God, Beautiful! Continue to flourish! And may you reap the good fruits from the Godly seeds you have sown (especially through these key elements and more) in Jesus name.

Chapter 13

The Main Factor

It is awesome to be bold and express our boldness in every area of our life, but our boldness doesn't mean anything without this main factor! Now, this is important to becoming bold! This main factor of being a bolder and better you is love. Love is the key to it all. Without love, God isn't present because God is love. When we include love into becoming a better version of ourselves, we invite God's Holy Spirit to transform us into the image of Jesus Christ. Within the book of the Corinthians in the Bible, the Apostle Paul shared a biblical blueprint to the church in Corinth. The foundation of this blueprint is love. Holy Spirit led Apostle Paul to describe what love is in chapter thirteen. Paul describes love as enduring with patience and serenity, kind and thoughtful, and much more (1 Cor. 13:4 AMP).

> Love endures with patience *and* serenity, love is kind *and* thoughtful, and is not jealous *or* envious; love does not brag and is not proud *or* arrogant. It is not rude; it is not self-seeking, it is not provoked [nor overly sensitive and easily angered]; it does not take into account a

> wrong *endured*. It does not rejoice at injustice, but rejoices with the truth [when right and truth prevail]. Love bears all things [regardless of what comes], believes all things [looking for the best in each one], hopes all things [remaining steadfast during difficult times], endures all things [without weakening]. Love never fails [it never fades nor ends].
> —1 Corinthians 13:4 – 8a AMP

Love creates stability in the different areas of our lives. Later in the New Testament, the Bible states that God is love (1 John 4:8). If we live from a place that excludes love, our foundation becomes shaky, and most likely, whatever we build will eventually break. In other words, if we build our lives other than Jesus Christ as our foundation, it will be unstable and not sustainable. My favorite teacher, preacher, and life coach, Jesus Christ, taught on the importance of building on a solid foundation (Matthew 7: 24 - 27). He also spoke on loving God, others, and ourselves (Matthew 22: 37-39).

Love does not gaslight, instead love highlights. Love highlights the good and the God in others and within ourselves. Sometimes love even highlights the wrongs in actions and finds redemptive solutions. Let's go back to the definition of love mentioned in first Corinthians chapter thirteen, and let's use it as a self-reflective tool to assess how we treat ourselves.

- Are we kind to ourselves? Are we patient with ourselves and God's process over our lives?
- Are we continually comparing ourselves to others or ourselves in past seasons? Are we jealous or envious?
- Are we prideful or humble? Are we self-seeking, or do we find ways to serve others?
- Are we easily irritable, easily offended, or resentful?

- Do we rejoice in wrongdoings, vengeance, or evil of any kind? Or do we rejoice in God's love, justice, and truth?
- Are we committed and faithful unto God? Do we hope for the best in Him, others, and ourselves with faith and holy expectation?
- Do we easily give up or endure difficult and great seasons in our lives by God's grace?

I would encourage all of us to study this passage of scripture in 1 Corinthians 13 and ask Holy Spirit to begin to give us new revelation about how we can love God, other people, and ourselves better. And also how we can receive genuine love from God and others better. In the places and spaces where we haven't love God, others and/or ourselves well, let us repent and ask God for forgiveness and continue walking with Jesus! Holy Spirit is a teacher of the anointing (John 14:26, 1 John 2:27). He is faithful to teach us how to be loving and compassionate to ourselves so that we can be loving and compassionate to others for God's glory alone.

Holy Spirit invites us to exude love, to express love to others and ourselves. One way we can express love to others is by first loving and honoring ourselves. Over the years, Holy Spirit taught me that we are called to love ourselves, not in a selfish, cultural view on self-love, but loving and honoring ourselves with kindness and compassion.

> But the Advocate, the Holy Spirit, whom the Father will send in My name, will teach you all things and will remind you of everything I have told you.
>
> —JOHN 14:26

Some practical ways Holy Spirit led me to love and be compassionate towards myself include: going on dates with God, lighting a candle and studying God's Word, journaling, writing two to three things I am grateful for at the end of the day, biblical mediation, being gracious and merciful to myself (especially after repenting), speaking positively and saying biblical truths over myself, having a spa day, and more! Holy Spirit is so creative that if we desire to grow in this or any area, He is able to give us unique ideas.

Although we each have our own perception of love, God's Word holds the true meaning of love. God's Word is the truth. In the words of Biblical teacher and author Lisa Bevere, "love without truth is a lie." Although there are many resources on the topic of love, The Word of God/ The Bible is the ultimate Source and gives us an insight on how to love. We should aim to put the Source, God's Spirit and His Word, above any resources we may have. And as we continue to share God's truth, let us do so in love. Pastor and Biblical Teacher Eric Mason once said, "truth without love is condemnation." We need both love and truth to help accurately articulate God's heart to others and to ourselves.

Many resources discuss expressing love within a productive and healthy matter. I came across some amazing resources in my journey of understanding healthy love, including *Boundaries* by Henry Cloud and John Townsend, *Five Love Language* by Gary Chapman, *Self-Love Workbook* by Tony A. Gaskins Jr, and *How We Love* by Milian & Kay Yerkovich. In addition to that, God also led me to powerful biblical communities through church and virtual online ministries (such as The One University) to display what healthy, Christ-like love looks like. There are so many more great books, e-courses, and resources to gain a more in-depth insight into the concept of healthy love. We can continue to ask God to send us people, biblical communities, and resources to walk as God's representatives of His love. Also, we can ask God to renew our minds to help us believe and receive healthy and loving relationships, including those we have with Him and ourselves.

By understanding God's love for us and embracing it, we can express love to one another! Also, when we dethrone the idols in our hearts and place Jesus at the center of our hearts, we can love one another better. Love can look like a variation of things to others. It can look like a gift, a listening ear, a hug, our comforting presence, and so many other things! Also, love can look like correction, a gentle redirection, or Holy Spirit convicting our hearts.

Another way we can embrace God's love for us is by going through therapy. Sometimes we are encouraged to go to therapy, but we are rarely encouraged to pray throughout our counseling journey. Holy Spirit is God, and He is also our Helper (John 14:26), He can lead us through our counseling journey. He can show us the roots of our issues, topics to focus on during counseling sessions, and so much more. He can also lead us to a counselor who displays healthy love attributes, respects us, someone who is efficient with our time, and can give us the tools and support we need.

Finding the right counselor with the leading of the Holy Spirit was one of the best decisions I've ever made. God began to reveal the codependency issues I had. And He led me to a counselor to walked me through my recovery process. If you feel led to find a therapist, I would encourage you to include Holy Spirit throughout your counseling journey. Pray unto God and ask him specific questions throughout your journey. He cares and loves you so much! He will never leave you or abandon you (Hebrews 13:5). It's so important to understand a healthy definition of love and find the appropriate help that we need to live out the healthy definition of love. Because once we begin to love out of a pure and clean heart through Jesus Christ, then we can really reflect God's love on this earth!

Experiencing and embracing God's perfect love for us through Jesus Christ is so fulfilling. There was a time in my life where I resisted God's love for me because of fear. Fear clouds our judgment and thought patterns. It can even lead to psychological and neurotically damage. Fear is an enemy to God's perfect love and surrendering unto Him. It may cause us to be controlling and hopeless in our lives. The devil tried to steal my faith in God, kill my hope, and destroy my trust in God's perfect love. But by God's divine grace, Jesus Christ and His saints have prayed for me that my faith will not fail and that after I repented I may strengthen you (see Luke 22:

31-32)! Hallelujah! God used what was meant for evil and turned it around for good and for His glory! The Scriptures say that perfect love expels all fear (1 John 4:18 NLT). Jesus is perfect love! And it is the power of God's perfect love that empowers us and equips us to shine bright for His glory!

Nowadays, I am abiding in God's perfect love for me. I am abiding in His presence and His peace. That peace is reminiscent of a cool breeze on a beautiful sandy beach while listening to the sound of the ocean waves. That peace that no matter what is going on, you can feel a calmness in your soul because your trust is in God! It is the peace that surpasses all human understanding (Phillippians 4:6). May you feel that same peace in your life, in Jesus name.

> Then you will experience God's peace, which exceeds anything we can understand. His peace will guard your hearts and minds as you live in Christ Jesus.
> —PHILIPPIANS 4:7

Love is so powerful and impactful; even babies can discern healthy love from their parents/caregivers. At a young age, babies begin to develop attachment styles based on how their parents love them. Many research shows how beneficial or adverse attachment styles are developed within children. These attachment styles carry throughout adulthood and affect how a person relates and expresses their love to others.

Sometimes we continue to carry the same attachment styles we had with our parents or caregivers and project it towards our relationship with God. But the truth is that God loves us more than our earthly parents ever could. Even Psalm 27 verse ten says, "even if my father and other abandon me, the LORD will hold me close" (Psalm 27:10 NLT). His love is so big, so vast, so abundant for us that it couldn't take a whole lifetime to comprehend fully. When we begin to see things through God's lens and point of view, we begin to elevate our perspective with His! The Scripture mentions how we are seated in heavenly places with Christ Jesus (Ephesians 2:6). When we begin to see ourselves, our situations, and our relationship with God through His lens, things begin to shift.

Holy Spirit wants to do something new within us! He wants to do something new through us and all around us! The truth is He is doing something new within us if we let Him! Let's pray to ask God to get rid of all the filth and everything that does not look like Him that was inside of us. Holy Spirit can do a spring cleaning in our heart and give us a clean heart (Psalm 51). Let us be in a position of humility and allow His consuming fire to burn everything that does not look like Jesus inside of us.

And let us invite Holy Spirit to rebuild and reconstruct those desolated places within us with His love, His joy, His peace, and His holy Word. He is the God who makes all things new. He is the Most High God, Lord of the breakthrough, breaking beyond every limitation on your life for your good and His glory! Let's continue to seek God's face, give Jesus our sacrifice of praise (Hebrews 13:15), walk out our obedience unto His Holy Spirit, and He will guide us into His truth and everlasting love.

> Look, I am about to do something new; even now it is coming. Do you not see it? Indeed, I will make a way in the wilderness, rivers in the desert.
>
> —Isaiah 43:19

In the process of surrendering to God, He taught me that I needed to trust Him to fully love Him. Without trust, there is no true and genuine love. I needed to trust that He will take care of my child and I, if I walk away from the toxic relationships with others and myself. I had to trust Him to believe Him when He proclaims how much He loves and wants to bless His children (Jeremiah 29:11, Psalm 84:11, Psalm 115:14 - 15). Walking our trusting and believing

God who He says He is, will make it easier to surrender to God's Holy Spirit and to be devoted to Him by His grace. He wants us to choose Him over the toxic cycle. Let us draw closer to God wholeheartedly, and He will draw near to us (James 4:8, Jeremiah 29:13).

Love is the main factor in being a bolder and better version of ourselves. Without it, we miss the essence of becoming bold in Jesus! Excluding authentic love is missing God altogether, for God is love (1 John 4:8). Love is also a part of surrendering to Holy Spirit. To be more loving is to surrender our hate. To be more forgiving is to surrender our pains. To become more compassionate is to surrender our apathy. To really live a life of surrender is to give up the fear, control, and anxieties. By surrendering those things to God's Holy Spirit, we look more like the One who loves us unconditionally, the One who is called our First Love because He loved us first (1 John 4:19, Revelation 2). By surrendering all of us unto Holy Spirit, we begin to look more like Jesus Christ.

Chapter 14

Living in His Light

Overcoming those dark seasons in my life was one of the hardest things I had to do. Because of God, not only did I come out of that season emotionally stronger, but I came out a better woman. I thank God for His love that protects me and uses what was meant for evil and turns it around for good and His glory (Genesis 50:20, Romans 8:28). God wants to do the same thing for you! May everything that was meant for evil in your life be turned around for good and for God's glory, in Jesus name! May God send you resources and destiny helpers through Christ Jesus to help you fulfill your holy calling, in Jesus name! May God look upon you with favor as you are in His presence and working with humility and excellence on your God-given assignments (Nehemiah 13:31c) in Jesus mighty name.

God wants to continue to show us the importance and the essential nature of seeing ourselves how God sees us, and seeing others how He sees them! The trauma you may experience in your life is not a period but a comma in your story. Jesus wants to write our stories through His goodness and love. Jesus is the author and finisher of our faith! By Jesus' love, we are living in His light, while walking out the callings and purpose He has for us. And I thank God for Jesus' love that He has for us and new mercies that continue to cover us! I pray that the eyes of our understanding be enlightened to see ourselves and others through the lenses of Jesus' redemptive love (Ephesians 1:18), in Jesus name…

> Jesus spoke to the people once more and said, "I am the light of the world. If you follow me, you won't have to walk in darkness, because you will have the light that leads to life."
> —John 8:12 NLT

Theroughout these past few years, God also showed me that I am not fighting against humans but against wicked spiritual armies (Ephesians 6 VOICE)! My ex wasn't my enemy, but that ungodly spirit that was operating within him is my enemy. I am not my enemy, but the spirit of fear and control that was operating within me is my enemy. People partners with the devil (knowingly or unknowingly) to bring forth evil. Overall, Jesus is the name above all names, and He holds all power in His hands! And Jesus not only began to reveal Himself to me as my Lord and Savior but also as My Defender and Deliverer! Jesus Christ is the One who defends and vindicates us! He is the One who delivers and heals us! He is the One who equips us!

As believers of Jesus Christ, the weapons we fight with are not tangible weapons but spiritual ones (2 Corinthians 10:4). As members of God's holy army, our weapons include:

- The Word of God/ the Bible (Ephesians 6:17)
- praying and fasting (Matthew 17:21)
- worship/obedience and praise (2 Chronicles 20, Isaiah 61:3)
- repentance and renunciation (Proverbs 28:13, Matthew 3:8)
- binding and loosing (Matthew 18:18)
- praying in the Holy Spirit (Ephesians 6:18, Jude 1:20)

- being a part of a healthy biblical community (Matthew 18:20, Hebrews 10:24-25)
- warring and praying through the tested prophetic words released over your life (1 Thessalonians 5:21-22, 1 Timothy 1:18)
- forgiving others (Matthew 18:21:35)
- putting on the Armor of God (Ephesians 6:13-17)
- testing every spirit (1 John 4:1)

And so much more! And other beautiful resources that help us walk out our deliverance includes obedience unto God, discipline, surrounding ourselves with Godly people, and so much more! I thank God for the spiritual weapons He provides for us. I also thank God for the natural resources to help protect us as well, such as boundaries, law enforcement, counselors, lawyers, restraining orders, etc. (If you or someone you know is in any type of danger, please seek help immediately). God wants us to use spiritual weapons as well as natural resources to protect, love, and honor ourselves effectively.

When we are in Christ, He calls us more than conquerors (Roman 8:37)! You are more than a conqueror in Christ Jesus! And remember that nothing can separate you from His love (Romans 8:38-29)! May you become a holy arrow of God's might, deliverance, and love here on this earth, in Jesus mighty name!

We are recipients of God's mercy and His grace, He gave us His Holy Spirit to guide us and look like Jesus Christ. In Jesus Christ, we learn how to persevere in the midst of crisis and trauma, knowing that He is faithful to love us, comfort us, and revive us!

There are many dynamics and levels of becoming a bolder and better version of ourselves. Boldness is not confined to one type of style. Our journey to becoming a bolder and better version of ourselves can be messy and unclear at first, but after finding the courage God gives us to continue the journey, we can embrace it! By speaking, submitting, and surrendering unto God and His will over our lives, we will come to witness many transformations in our heart, mind, body, and soul!

The escape plan of speaking, submitting, and surrendering unto God did not lead me to become a better and bolder version of myself, it was the Spirit of God that ultimately did that! It was Holy Spirit who led me to seek Jesus and journey with Him in His Word. He led me to pray God's will and His Word over my life in the secret place of prayer. I learned that the secret place of prayer is a powerful tool in my life. I went from living in a place of rejection and toxic environments to flourishing and abiding in Jesus' love and light. This divine transformation began in a place of prayer. Holy Spirit gave me this plan for the drastic change He did in my life! This transformation did not happen overnight, and God's escape plan for you may not be the same escape plan that He gave me, and that's okay. May we continue to be open to how God wants to move within our lives.

Wherever we are in life, we can speak to our Heavenly Father and speak the Word of God over us and those around us. We can submit to Jesus Christ as our Lord and Savior and the journey He has for us. Also, we are invited to surrender our lives unto Holy Spirit. Holy Spirit is a beautiful gift. Author and Pastor Michael Todd mentioned that Holy Spirit is the upgrade in our faith walk. Once we are believers in Christ Jesus, we can sincerely ask Father God for Holy Spirit in our lives if we like (Luke 11:13). Our lives are tremendously better with Holy Spirit in it! I can write another book full of more testimonies of how Holy Spirit enhances my life and my faith walk with Jesus Christ. He is my ultimate Helper. Comforter, Strategist, and CEO. Holy Spirit is truly my best friend!

Soak in His presence, Beautiful. Remember, we do have access to God through the salvation and blood of Jesus Christ! I heard a preacher once said that the blood of Jesus Christ is like the red carpet to the Throne of God! The blood of Jesus Christ calls for the forgiveness of our sins. Don't let any sin keep you from entering into the presence of God. As believers of Jesus Christ, we can simply repent and continue to enter in God's presence. Enter in a beautiful time of prayer with Him. There is no shame or guilt in God's presence, King Jesus already paid the penalty for that on the cross. Christ has redeemed us! Jesus is our holy lawyer, our advocate, who prays on our behalf in heaven (Romans 8:34). Enter in! Your access has been granted…

> Let us therefore come boldly to the throne of grace, that we may obtain mercy and find grace to help in time of need.
> —Hebrews 4:16 NKJV

May you find healing and wholeness as you begin or continue your journey into becoming a bolder and better version of yourself in God, in Jesus name! God doesn't do no halfway work. There are some popular saying that says, "if He brought you to it, He'll get you through it" and "He doesn't place more on you than you can bear." That's not always the case. Sometimes God does place more on us than we can bear (that specific bible verse in 1 Corinthians 10:13 is referring to temptations). Sometimes God can use life circumstances that are bigger than us as an invitation to get to know another perspective of Him. In one season, we may know Him as a Savior, but now He may introduce Himself to us as our Lord/Leader. In another season, we may know Him as a teacher, but now maybe He wants to invite us to know Him as our Healer and Miracle Worker and so on.

I never would've thought I would survive an abusive relationship as an adult. Everything that I survived wasn't by my strength or boldness, but it was by God's strength and grace. By His grace, be fully present to raise my son in a healthy and loving environment. Also, I can use my voice to testify of God's faithfulness and goodness! And by His grace, I am not only surviving, but I am thriving and flourishing into the woman God called me to be! And He wants to do the same for you!

God does not only want you to survive what you're going through, but He wants you to thrive and flourish within Him! You are beautiful, you are loved, you are honored, and you are special in the eyes of God! He wants to commune with you day in and day out! He is inviting you to dive deeper in His perfect love.

If you have something to work through, confront, forgive, etc., start working on it. You are not alone. When you are in Christ, there are more for you than against you (2 Kings 6:16, Romans 8:31)! I know it can be hard, but know that God is with you no matter how anything in your past or present looks like! God has placed ambassadors of His love and grace around you! Sometimes you may meet those ambassadors in unusual ways. You will make it through with God and by following His instructions! Continue to run your race with endurance! And when you make it through, may you become ambassadors of God's love and grace to others!

In 2015, Pixar created a movie called *Inside Out*. It is my son's and I favorite movie. The movie is about Riley, a young girl who moves to a new town and starts a new school. With the new adventures that await her, the movie displays the different emotions that live in the control center of her mind. Each emotion is a character, such as Joy, Anger, Sadness, and more. As each emotion interacts with one another, they also determine Riley's mood for the day and her response to the circumstances she faces. A dramatic change happens to Riley as two of the main emotions become lost outside of the control center. The change in Riley's behavior directly reflects the missing emotions in the control center within herself. The movie continues to track the adventures of Riley and her different emotions.

This movie was really interesting. While watching the movie, I began to question: who is the control center of my mind and heart? Is it my emotions, is it my past, or is it God's Holy Spirit that is calling the shots? Does my behavior towards God and others reflect that Jesus Christ sits on the throne of my heart? Does my thoughts and actions reflect that Jesus Christ is in the control center of my mind? This is the time to invite God's Holy Spirit to reexamine our hearts and minds and ask ourselves, *who or what is running the control center of our heart and mind?*

> Trust in the LORD with all your heart; do not depend on your own understanding. Seek His will in all you do, and he will show you which path to take.
>
> —PROVERBS 3:5-6 NLT

Never let shame, fear, or anything else hold you back from being all God has called you to be! This is not the time to shrink back from God's calling over our lives but to walk boldly and unapologetically in it! We can take it a few steps at a time according to however the Holy Spirit is leading us. The Word mentions how God directs our path when we acknowledge Him in all of our ways (Proverb 3:6)! Let us continue to walk boldly in the image He called us to walk into. Our redemption comes with responsibility. Thank God for His infinite love and grace He equips us with to handle those responsibilities. If God calls you to it, He will equip you through it! We are not called to live an apathetic life in Jesus Christ while neglecting the needs of others (see Amos 6:1). God is calling us to live a life of holy compassion and servanthood unto Him and others. You are not reading this book by coincidence or by chance, but God knew the right timing for you to read this book and to receive empowerment from Him.

As I mentioned earlier, whether you see yourself like me, Sarah, Janah, Valerie, or Gregory in my story, if you're reading this now, God has a glorious and redemptive plan for you! Yes, YOU! I even heard right now 'repent and enter into times of refreshing' (Acts 3:19). Repent means simply turn away. Turn away from everything in your life that is not of Jesus Christ and turn to Him. He loves you so much! Receive His love and experience the endless and limitless love He has for you. Yes, walking with Jesus (and continually choosing to walk with Him), even as His follower, isn't easy, but it is the boldest decision you can ever make, and it is worth it! I pray that God will equip you with enduring faith unto Him, and you will begin to dream with God and that your vision is clear, in Jesus name.

> For the LORD God is our sun and our shield. He gives us grace and glory. The LORD will withhold no good thing from those who do what is right.
>
> —PSALM 84:11

May God withhold no good thing from you as you continue to do what is right, in Jesus name! Thanks be to God for remaining to be faithful, for His holy restoration, and giving us Jesus Christ and His Holy Spirit! That we may speak, submit, and surrender unto Him! For making us into a new creation in Christ! God saw us dying to sin and called us declared that we may LIVE! That we may find life within Jesus and truly LIVE (John 3:16, John 10:10b). His hope is that we choose to live like Jesus lived and is still living, that we may embrace the better and bolder version of ourselves in Christ by the leading of Holy Spirit!

> I have come that they may have life, and that they may have *it* more abundantly.
>
> —JOHN 10:10B NKJV

Looking back at my life, I am so grateful God used me to share His words and encouragement with you. No attack, no warfare, no shame, nothing can make me feel regretful of the fact that I am God's daughter and vessel through the salvation of Jesus Christ! In fact, what I went through in those dark days was meaningful to me because it taught me to pay attention to God and His Holy Word (Psalm 119:71 NLT). Now I am living in Jesus' light!

My life is a testimony to God's love, mercy, and faithfulness. God is using me, my story, and my brokenness to help serve someone else. He used me, someone who lived in the shadows of rejection, trauma, recklessness, someone who was addicted to food and sex, went through abusive relationships with others and with herself. And yet, He still chose to use me! He still chose me to be His daughter, to be a friend and disciple of Jesus Christ, to follow and to inhabit His Holy Spirit, and to be a part of His people! He chose me to be a reflection of His love, joy, and light and share the Gospel of Jesus Christ with others. He made beauty from the ashes in my life (Isaiah 41:3), and I am truly grateful to Him! He turned my cries of mourning into cries of rejoicing.

No matter what you've been through, God still wants to choose you! He is calling you from being a victim to victorious in Jesus Christ! He wants to make beauty from the pain within your life! God wants to turn your cries of mourning into times of rejoicing! He is calling you to survive, to thrive, and then to FLOURISH for His glory alone! As this world is getting darker and darker until Jesus Christ comes back, He is calling you to shine brighter and brighter in Him! No matter what is happening around us, Holy Spirit wants to partner with you! The time is now to walk out your identity and calling in Christ Jesus! The time is now to be unashamed of your past and surrender it all unto God! The time is now to arise and shine for Christ's glory alone (Isaiah 60:1-3, Matthew 5:14). Take it one step at a time, God is with you every step of the way Sis. If you are reading or listening to this right now, I want you to know that He chose you to be a part of His redemptive love story! The question is: will you choose Him?

> For at one time, you were darkness, but now you are light in the Lord. Walk as children of light.
> —Ephesians 5:8

Yasss! Congratulations! You made it to the end of this book! Thank you for choosing this book to be a part of your life's journey! I pray it was an edifying and strengthening resource for you! Blessings!

Prayer

I pray that you were blessed while going through this journey of becoming a bolder and better version of yourself. It is an honor to have this book be a part of your beautiful journey! Thank you for reading this book. Before we end the book, if you don't mind, can I pray for you?

Papa God, thank You for being loving, kind, mighty, and holy! There is no one like You (Psalm 86:8)! Thank You for loving us so much and giving us Your precious Son, Jesus Christ, to die for us. We repent, Papa, for rejecting Jesus, which ultimately meant we rejected you. There is only one way to be with you, Papa, and it's through your Son, Jesus! And we repent for every sin (known and unknown), every thought, and action that did not reflect the name and character of Jesus Christ! Create in us a clean heart and renew a loyal spirit within us (Psalm 51:10).

Papa, I ask that You be with every reader, or listener, of this book right now. I pray that You may open their heart so that they may receive Your perfect love! Deliver us and heal us, O God, from everything that is not of You! In the Name of Jesus, break every hindrance holding us back from flourishing in Jesus Christ. Turn every curse on your child's life into a Godly blessing just like You did for the children of Israel as mentioned in Nehemiah 13:2. Bind up every spirit that is not Holy Spirit within us and around us and cast it to hell. Papa, loose Your Spirit, Holy Spirit, within us and holy, Jesus Christ worshipping angels around us. Loose Your power, loose Your perfect love, loose your sound mind with us, Papa! Destroy every demonic delay, distraction, deception, and every demonic work that

Prayer

is assigned to our lives, Papa God, with Your consuming fire. For You, Papa God is a consuming fire (Hebrews 12:29 BSB)

Fill our hearts with Your love, truth, wisdom, understanding, and boldness! Help us to chooses what pleases You God over what pleases our flesh. Help us to choose freedom in Christ over comfortability! Help us to choose faith over fear! For Your Word says in John 8:36, if the Son sets us free then we are FREE INDEED! So, in the name of Jesus Christ, I speak FREEDOM over every area in my sister's life! FREEDOM, FREEDOM, FREEDOM, in the mighty name of Jesus Christ! I pray for divine restoration over my sister's heart, mind, soul, relationships, and resources in Jesus name! She is beautiful! She is blessed! And I thank You, Papa, for her life!

Lord Jesus, please release heavenly wisdom, insight, strategies, and instructions for my sister's life (James 1:5, Proverbs 16:16). May she work with love and faithfulness, may she find favor with You and with others, and may she prosper in her God-given callings and assignments according to Proverb 3:4-5 and Psalm 90:17 in Your timing Papa. Help us to exemplify Your life in unimaginable ways, above what we can ask, think, or imagine according to the power that is working within us (Ephesians 3:20). Be exalted in our mind, King Jesus! Be exalted in our hearts, King Jesus, and be exalted in our souls! Show us how we can speak to you, Papa God, and to speak your Word over those around us and ourselves. Give us the wisdom to submit to You Lord Jesus, and show us how to surrender all of us unto Your Holy Spirit. Not our wills, but let Yours be done in our lives (Luke 22:42).

Lord, show us Your personalized escape plan for our lives, whether we are escaping toxic relationships, toxic habits, old careers, etc. Cover us with your feathers and may we take refuge under your wings according to Psalm 91:4. Lord Jesus, please send Your holy angels to protect us as we are going through this time of transition. May You God block every weapon formed, against my sister, from succeeding according to Isaiah 54:17a. Help us see others how You see them and help us see ourselves how You see us, through the lens of redemptive love and holy truth!

May mercy, peace, and love be multiplied to every reader, every listener, every partner of this book, according to Jude 1:2. May we go out and tell someone else about your amazing love, grace, and Gospel of Jesus Christ. May we go out and make disciples of Jesus Christ like You instructed us to in Matthew 28. And may You get all the glory, honor, and praise for the work You are doing in us and through us, Lord Jesus! The grace of the Lord Jesus Christ, and the love of God, and the fellowship of the Holy Spirit be with you (2 Corinthians 13:14). We pray all these things in the matchless, mighty, and glorious name of Jesus Christ! Amen!

Resources Page

This is a list of helpful resources based on topics discussed within this book. Some of these resources may be based solely in the United States. This list of resources is not a part of any sponsorships or paid advertisements associated with this book and publisher. I hope that any one of these resources will help and/or equip you for this journey call life. Blessings!

The YouVersion Bible App
www.youversion.com

Life Application Study Bible
tyndale.com/sites/lasb

Biblical Meditation App
Abide Bible Meditation & Sleep

Online Parallel Bible
www.biblehub.com

National Domestic Violence Hotline
1 800 787 SAFE (7233)
Thehotline.org

Women Against Abuse
1 (866) 723 – 3014
womenagainstabuse.org

NATIONAL SUICIDE PREVENTION LIFELINE

1-800-273-8255 (TALK)
www.suicidepreventionlifeline.org

Faithful Counseling / Therapy
faithfulcounseling.com

To find a personal mentor or coach, visit:
MyMentor.life

PODCASTS

She's Up GANG
By Angela Hicks

The Amanda Ferguson Show
By Amanda Ferguson

Real Talk Kim
By Kimberly Jones

The Codependency No More Podcast
By Brian Pisor

He Restores My Soul with Jani Ortlund
By Jani Ortlund

BOOKS

Whisper: How to Hear the Voice of God
By Mark Batterson

Forgiveness: A Coloring Journal Supporting
Your Journey to Freedom
By Courtney B. Dunlap

Boundaries: When to Say Yes, How to Say
No to Take Control of Your Life
By Henry Cloud and John Townsend

Safe People: How to Find Relationships That Are
Good for You and Avoid Those That Aren't
By Henry Cloud and John Townsend

Self-Love Workbook
By Tony Gaskins Jr.

Fervent: A Woman's Battle Plan to Serious,
Specific and Strategic Prayer
By Priscilla Shirer

Unleashed: Being Conformed to the Image of Christ
By Dr. Eric Mason

The Ruth Anointing: Becoming a Woman
of Faith, Virtue, and Destiny
By Michelle McClain-Walters

100 Days of Believing Bigger
By Marshawn Evans Daniels

21 Days of Preparation
By Adrian D. Davis

Biblical Declarations

I was made through the image of God (Genesis 1:27 NKJV)

God will instruct me and teach me in the way I should go: He will guide me with His eye. (Psalm 32:8 NKJV)

I can do anything through Christ who strengthens me (Philippians 4:13 NKJV)

The Lord is my helper, I will not be afraid (Psalm 118:6 NKJV)

I am a child of God, and I am called for such a time as time (Galatians 3:26, Esther 4:14b, 1 Peter 2:9 NKJV)

God lives within me; I will not fall. I will praise You, for I am fearfully *and* wonderfully made; Marvelous are Your works, And *that* my soul knows very well. (Psalm 46:5, Psalm 139:14 NKJV)

Do not be afraid or discouraged, for the Lord will personally go ahead of me. He will be with me; He will neither fail me nor abandon me (Deuteronomy 31:8 NKJV)

God has not given me a spirit of fear, but I am filled with God's power, His love, and a sound mind (2 Timothy 1:7 NKJV)

No weapons formed against my family and I shall prosper (Isaiah 54:17a NKJV)

May the LORD give me increase more and more, me and my children. May I be blessed by the LORD, Who made heaven and earth. (Psalm 115:14 – 15 NKJV)

He who is in me is greater than he who is in the world (1 John 4:4b NKJV)

I pray and declare all these things in the name of Jesus Christ

Acknowledgments

I want to thank God for my baby (who is not a baby anymore), my ugga-mugga, my son, C.J.! You are my perfect gift from God, and I am so grateful and honored to be your mama! I love being your mama! Your smile and sense of humor brighten up every room you enter and my heart. I pray the Lord will continue to be with you, in you, and all around you. And that God's mercy, peace, and love be multiplied to you all the days of your life (Jude 1:2), and that you will give Him all the glory, honor, and praise. I love you, I adore you, and I honor you C!

To my mother, Adeline: Thank you for always telling me to "dream big" as a young girl. Thank you for listening to me as a teen. Thank you for supporting and loving me as an adult. All of your investment has not and will not go in vain, in Jesus name! You are THE BEST mom and grandma I could ask for, and we thank God for you! I am so glad the Lord picked me to be your daughter. I love you and our relationship, Madre. Thank you for always supporting my dreams and visions. And most importantly, thank you Madre for all that you are and all that you do! I truly appreciate and love you!

To my father, Pierre: Thank you for always loving me and supporting me. I love and honor you Papi! Your boldness in life and sense of structure have an impact on me. Thank you for always being you and a joy to me and C.J.! The Lord has created you to be hard-working, funny, diligent, and innovative, and I thank God He picked me to inherit those qualities within you! I thank God for you! I love and honor you!

Acknowledgments

To the memory of my late brother, Sebastien. I was privileged to be Sebastien's sister. He showed me it doesn't matter how young you are; I can become bold and loving at any age! His legacy will live in my heart! Continue to rest well with our Heavenly Father, Seby Boy. We love you!

To my family & friends: Grandma Sylvia, Aunt Rose & Uncle Daniel, and Gigi and Uncle Louis, Gloria, Jean, Kayla, Rose, Michael, Vanessa, Kevin, Richard, Sierra, Norme, Alens, Ayiana & Aaron, Courtney, Sharni, Funmi, Angela, Ty, Gerni, Tupu, Lola, Taiye, Becky, Jay, Shannon, Pascale, Shalita, Benita, Raaya, De'Andrea, Taisje, Mary, Tammira, Lauren, Shonda, Josiah, The Browns, Daphne, Franceska, The Alfords, Emily, Natalie, Andrea, Brandy, and every single person in my life! Thank you for loving me and praying for me! Your love and kindness in my life are a blessing from our Heavenly Father and I am so grateful for each of you! It's an honor to be in your life. I love yall!

To the editor of this book and sister in the faith, Casey Potter: your listening ear has helped heal my heart! Thank you for being an amazing friend and editor. And thank you for editing this book and doing it all while being an amazing wife and mother to your family! I thank God for you, Sis! Love you!

To the cover designer of this book and my sister in Christ, Gloria O. I thank God for you and your heart, patience, and tenacity. It is an honor to work with you for this project! Your diligience inspired me throughout this journey. You are truly a blessing in our lives! Love you!

To my Pastors and their families: Dr. Eric Mason and Lady Yvette Mason, Pastor Curtis Dunlap, Pastor Nyron Burke, Pastor Gueshill Wharwood, Pastor Vernon Mobley Jr, Pastor Mac Lawhorn, Pastor Mark Lyons

To my Ministry Leaders: - Dr. Sarita Lyons, Tamika Sloan, and Alexis Moses, Community at Epiph – my family in NELG, my SALTy Sistas, Youth Ministry, and everyone at Epiphany Fellowship. Your support, endless sacrifices, guidance, and love reflects Christ's lovingkindness, mercy, and grace on earth. By God's grace, I thank God for your prayers, love, and kindness that carried me through the darkest valleys in my life. I thank God for your consistent love, care, leadership, sound teachings, comfort, wise counsel, and encouragement. I thank God for Epiphany Fellowship and for each and every one of you! And thank you for cultivating my character and leading me to look more like Jesus every day. By God's grace, I will continue to show off the glory of Christ in every area of my life. I love and honor you all!

Thank you to every one of my brothers, sisters, and mentors in the Body of Christ. To Mareena, Chimere, Jamil, Sherie, Pastor Edwin Francois and Lady Quiarra Francois, Prophetess Sukha Williams, Olivia, everyone in New Dimensions Christian Outreach, Pastor Cierra Kemp and Pastor AK, First Lady Joelle, Prophetess Erica, Prophetess Markiya, Prophetess Kisha Cephas, Melanie, JimDre, Pastor Manford and Lady Shaida, Sister Lavetta everyone in The Restoration House, Dr. Delanie Smith and everyone in BAM empowerment, and everyone who encouraged me in my walk with Jesus and this book writing journey within these past few years! I thank Jesus for His beautiful Bride, and it is an honor to be a part of His Church. I love y'all!

Thank you to all the youth in youth min., all the kids in Kidz min. my mentee, CC, you all are full of zeal and remind me to stay on fire for Jesus! God is doing amazing things within your generation! May the Lord continue to bless you and equip you for such a time as this, in Jesus' mighty name! I love you but always remember Jesus loves you more!

To every person in the Body of Christ: May God's mercy, peace, and love be multiplied to you according to Jude 1:2, in Jesus name! I love you Family!

And last but absolutely not least, to my Lord and Savior Jesus Christ: Thank you for not giving up on me, even when I gave up on myself. Thank you for loving me when I wasn't lovable, caring for me when I was stubborn, forgiving me when I was rebellious and repented, counseling me, and so much more. You heard my cries, You listened to my questions, You taught me how to be loving, courageous, kind, better, and bold. You taught me to be more like You! You lead me, You love me, You cover me, You redeem me and call me your own. For this, I am forever grateful! I love you, Lord. Thank You for using me to spread this message of the Gospel and to advance Your kingdom! Be glorified in my life!

Thank you to Papa God for giving us Your only Son to died and overcome sin and death for our iniquities! Thank You for being so gracious and loving! Thank You for loving me for me, and letting your love affirm me time and time again, for letting your love transform me, time and time again. Thank You for choosing me to be a part of your kingdom and for being a good, gracious Father! You are amazing Papa! I love and honor you!

Thank you to my Leader, and best friend Holy Spirit! You are My everything! You are glorious and wonderful! Thank you for imparting your creativity, showing me new words and scriptures as I wrote this book, giving me sentences and sayings, comforting me when I felt alone writing, for healing me and so much more. Thank you for seeing me, delivering me, and healing me! Thank You being my best friend! You are so good! Thank You Holy Ghost for always pointing my heart to Jesus! Have Your way in my life Holy Spirit in Jesus mighty name!

Notes

Chapter 2 Face to Face

1) More information on domestic violence
   www.thehotline.org.

2) Cambridge Dictionary
   https://dictionary.cambridge.org/us/dictionary/english/multifaceted
   Definition of **multifaceted** from the **Cambridge Advanced Learner's Dictionary & Thesaurus** © Cambridge University Press

3) Ruby
   Ruby gemstone
   https://www.britannica.com/topic/ruby
   CONTRIBUTOR:
   The Editors of Encyclopaedia Britannica
   TITLE
   Ruby
   PUBLISHER
   Encyclopædia Britannica
   DATE PUBLISHED
   April 16, 2020

Chapter 4 – Unmuzzled

1) Definition of grace
Merriam-Webster, Incorporated. (2021). Grace. Retrieved January 13, 2021, from https://www.merriam-webster.com/dictionary/grace

2) Definition of mercy
Merriam-Webster, Incorporated. (2021). Mercy. Retrieved January 13, 2021, from https://www.merriam-webster.com/dictionary/mercy

Chapter 6

Trauma - Dictionary.com. (n.d.). *Trauma definition & meaning*. Dictionary.com. Retrieved October 4, 2021, from https://www.dictionary.com/browse/trauma.
Triumph
"Prevail." *Merriam-Webster.com Dictionary*, Merriam-Webster, https://www.merriam-webster.com/dictionary/prevail. Accessed 4 Oct. 2021

Chapter 8 – Stand Out in Character

"Character." Merriam-Webster.com Dictionary, Merriam-Webster, https://www.merriam-webster.com/dictionary/character. Accessed 19 Jul. 2021.

Chapter 11 – Prudence and Purpose

"Prudence." Merriam-Webster.com Dictionary, Merriam-Webster, https://www.merriam-webster.com/dictionary/prudence. Accessed 22 Aug. 2021.

Chapter 12 – The Keys

1) Cambridge Dictionary
   https://dictionary.cambridge.org/us/dictionary/english/humility
   Definition of **humility** from the **Cambridge Advanced Learner's Dictionary & Thesaurus** © Cambridge University Press

Author Contact Page

Author's name: Kimberly Sanon
Author's Website: KimberlySanon.com

E-mail: admin@KimberlySanon.com

Facebook: Kimberly Sanon
Twitter: Kimberly Sanon
Instagram: @KimberlySanon
Youtube: Kimberly Sanon
Linkedin: Kimberly Sanon
Linkedin Link: https://www.linkedin.com/in/kimberlysanon/

For coaching sessions, please visit: Mymentor.life/KimberlySanon

Publisher's information:
Equipping Arrows Enterprise, LLC.
EquippingArrowsEnterprise.com
Email: admin@equippingarrowsenterprise.com

Made in the USA
Middletown, DE
11 May 2022

65612227R00069